To Dr. and Mrs. Doughtie,

   We have greatly appreciated and enjoyed you this "first" semester, and we look forward to many wonderful semesters to come.

   Merry Christmas!

   —The Members of Will Rice College

RICE UNIVERSITY
A 75th ANNIVERSARY PORTRAIT

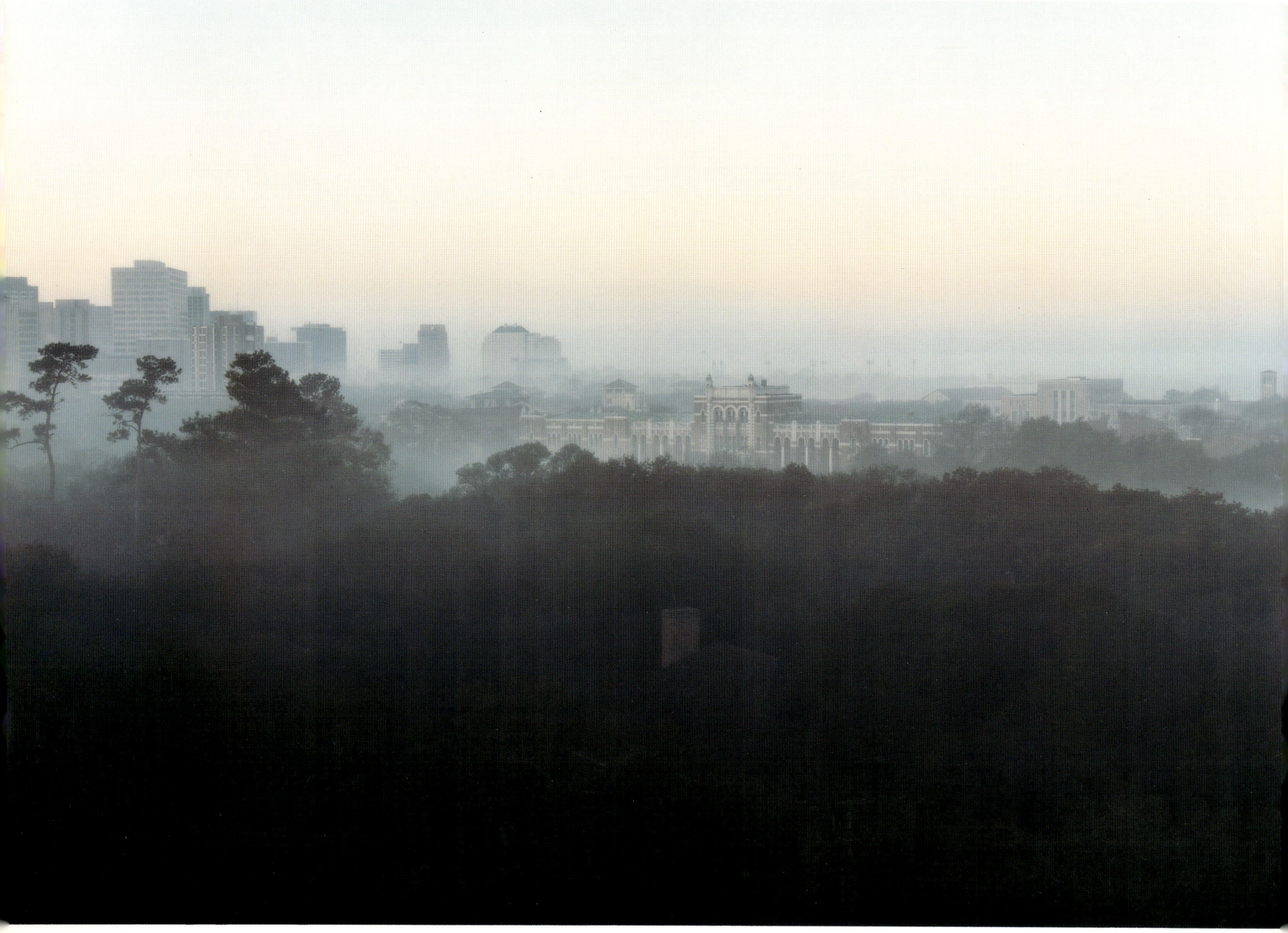

RICE UNIVERSITY
A 75th ANNIVERSARY PORTRAIT

PHOTOGRAPHS BY GEOFF WINNINGHAM

HISTORICAL NARRATIVE BY JOHN B. BOLES
COMMENTARY BY FRYAR CALHOUN

RICE UNIVERSITY PRESS
HOUSTON

Copyright © 1987 by Rice University
Photographs © 1987 by Geoff Winningham
All rights reserved
First Edition, 1987
Printed in Japan
Requests for permission to reproduce material from
this work should be addressed to:
Rice University Press
Post Office Box 1892
Houston, Texas 77251

Library of Congress Catalog Card Number 87-60696
ISBN-0-89263-265-8

Construction of the Administration Building of the Rice Institute, 1911 (facing page)

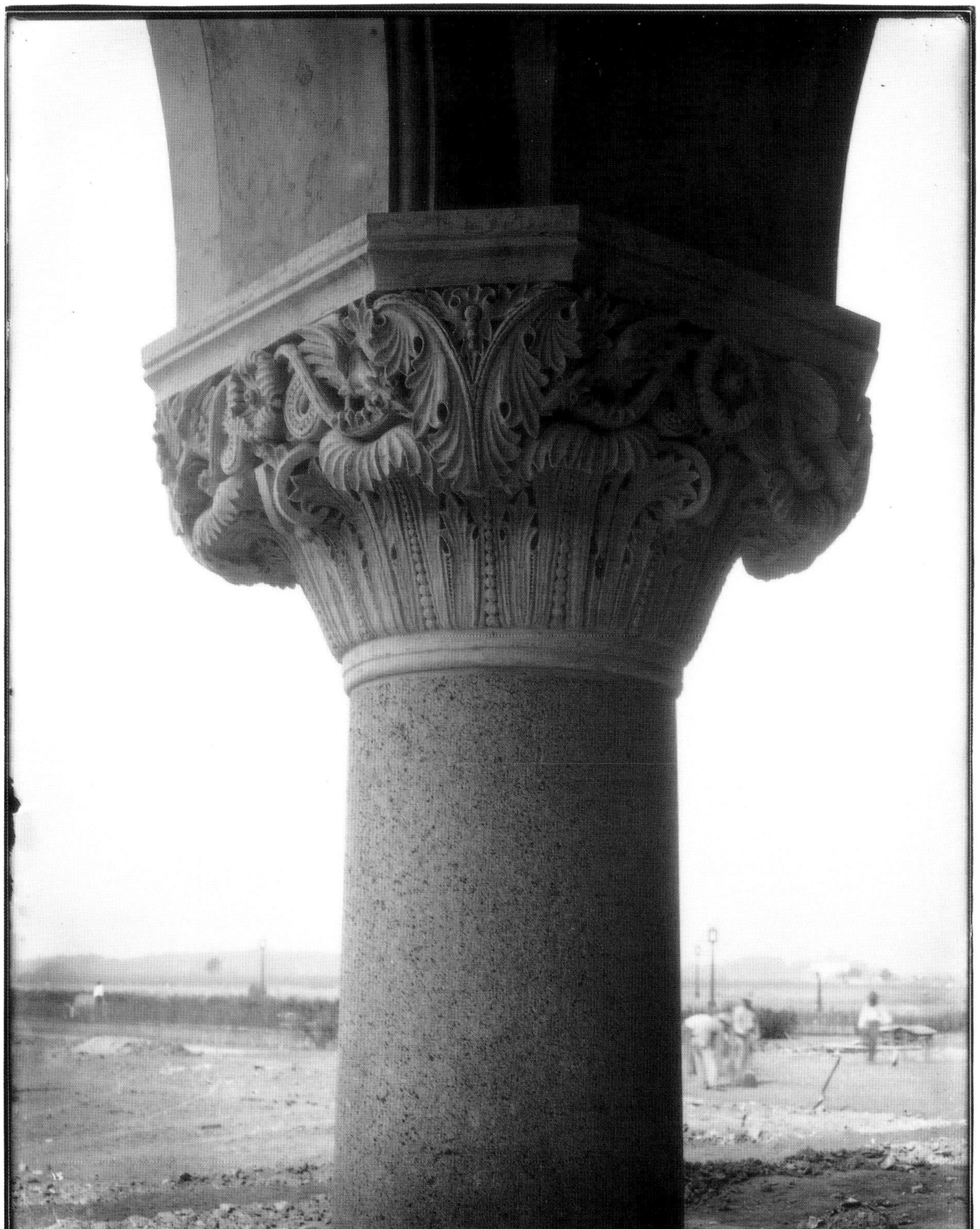

An old photograph of the Rice Institute's opening ceremonies in 1912 helps to put the early ambitious plans in perspective. Twin columns of academic dignitaries in cap and gown, some the delegates of great European and American universities, march down a rutted track across a featureless plain. Their unseen goal, the school's first building, must have looked like a boundary marker at the edge of the civilized world.

The Rice Institute was so far west of Houston, then a town of fewer than a hundred thousand souls, that the road that became South Main was still unpaved. A "Toonerville" trolley line had to be constructed to ferry students and the public to its gates. The sprawling campus had just been stitched together from a patchwork of flat, low-lying farms along a mosquito-ridden bayou. Until the last stubborn farmer gave in and moved shortly before the ceremonies, it appeared that the inaugural procession would have to be rerouted to avoid passing right by his pigsty.

Other photos from those early days show the black-robed scholars' destination: an elegant brick and marble fantasy of cloisters, columns, and portals, Romanesque in inspiration and Renaissance in rhythm, rising out of the muddy prairie. Inside, vaulted studies, a library, and a paneled faculty chamber recalled Ivy league neo-Gothic as well as the real version at Oxford and Cambridge. Outside, faces and figures on stone plaques and intricately carved capitals represented letters, science, art, and masters of university disciplines from history (Thucydides) to medicine (Pasteur).

The main administration and academic building, later named Lovett Hall for Rice's first president, was no Spartan housing for a plain little trade school, but an ambitious architectural statement that could be read as a program for the infant institution. It was the first mark on a blank canvas, an imposing shard of instant history driven into the surface of a new land that had little.

—*Fryar Calhoun*

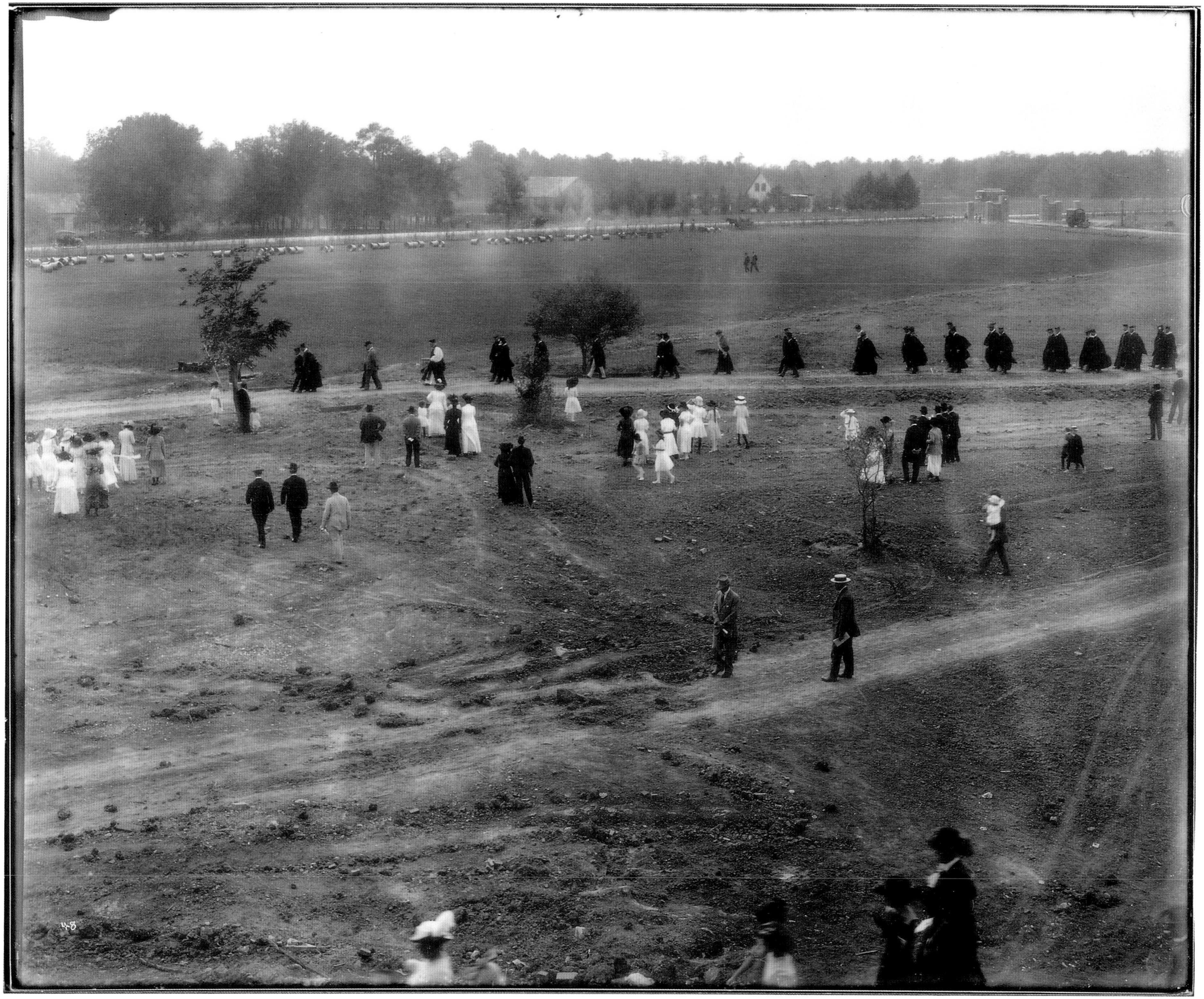
48

Seen from an upper-floor window of Rice University's library in the late afternoon, Lovett Hall takes on a magical quality. Its pinkish bricks become warmer and redder, its tiles and mosaics and marbles more deeply colored, and its windows diamond-like in the reflected light. With the hedges, manicured lawn, and pebbled walks in the foreground, the lush forest of dark-green live oaks rolling out behind it, and, on the horizon, the gleaming office towers of downtown Houston, the effect is stunning. Although the Rice campus sits squarely in the midst of the boom and bustle of modern-day Houston, it has an aura of quiet beauty and stability that seems somehow eternal, as though it is in this world but not of it. Therein lies the enduring charm of Rice that captivated its initial visitors in 1912 and gives today's observer a sense of its special character.

In 1912 Rice had one general-purpose academic building (now called Lovett Hall), one laboratory building, two residence halls, a commons building for student and faculty dining, and a campus of almost 300 acres of treeless plains. Beyond the indistinct boundaries of the campus there were some pines to the south, toward what is now Hermann Park; in other directions, one saw nothing except, perhaps, cattle grazing in the distance. At the far western edge of the campus there meandered a stream known as Harris Gully, where biology professor Julian Huxley and his assistant, Joseph Davies, came to collect laboratory specimens—and where Huxley first encountered swimming grasshoppers and the mud chimneys of crayfish. The campus lay beyond the southwestern fringes of Houston, an adolescent city of about 90,000 people. The paving stopped a mile or so before Main Street reached the school. Here, on a flat, flood-prone expanse of prairie—"a level and stupid site," campus architect Ralph Adams Cram called it—President Edgar Odell Lovett envisioned a great university, one boldly planted in a region not noted for nurturing academic enterprise.

For all the sense of adventure with which President Lovett launched the infant university—"on the anniversary of Columbus' arrival," he said in his inaugural address in October 1912, "we too are setting out on a voyage of discovery"—no university had a more precarious beginning. William Marsh Rice had come from Massachusetts to Houston in 1839, and, since he possessed a shrewd business sense, his fortune grew with the frontier town. Even the Civil War did not disrupt his accumulation of wealth, for he temporarily moved to Matamoros, Mexico, where he traded in cotton despite the Union blockade. After the war Rice returned north, and for the remainder of his life he lived in New York City and on a nearby farm in New Jersey. Rice maintained his business interests in Houston, returning often to supervise his far-flung activities. Twice married but childless, Rice sometime in his sixties apparently began to think about what he would leave to posterity. In 1882 he drew up a will leaving the bulk of his estate to an orphans' institute to be established on his New Jersey farm property. And that home for parentless children might have been William Marsh Rice's legacy to the ages save for a fortuitous conversation in the late 1880s with Houston businessman Cesar M. Lombardi, who suggested that since Rice had made his fortune in Houston, there could be no more appropriate monument to his memory than a building for a municipal high school. Cautious by nature, Rice promised to give the idea careful consideration.

Visiting Houston again in the late spring of 1891, Rice told his attorney, Captain James A. Baker, that he had decided to endow not a high school but a separate establishment to be called the William Marsh Rice Institute for the Advancement of Literature, Science, and Art. On May 13, 1891, Rice signed a deed of indenture with six trustees incorporating the new university. The following year Rice gave the institute several parcels of land, and in 1896, after his second wife's death, he wrote a new will leaving the bulk of his fortune to the Institute. By Rice's instructions, nothing else was to be done until after his death.

Northwest façade, Administration Building, 1912

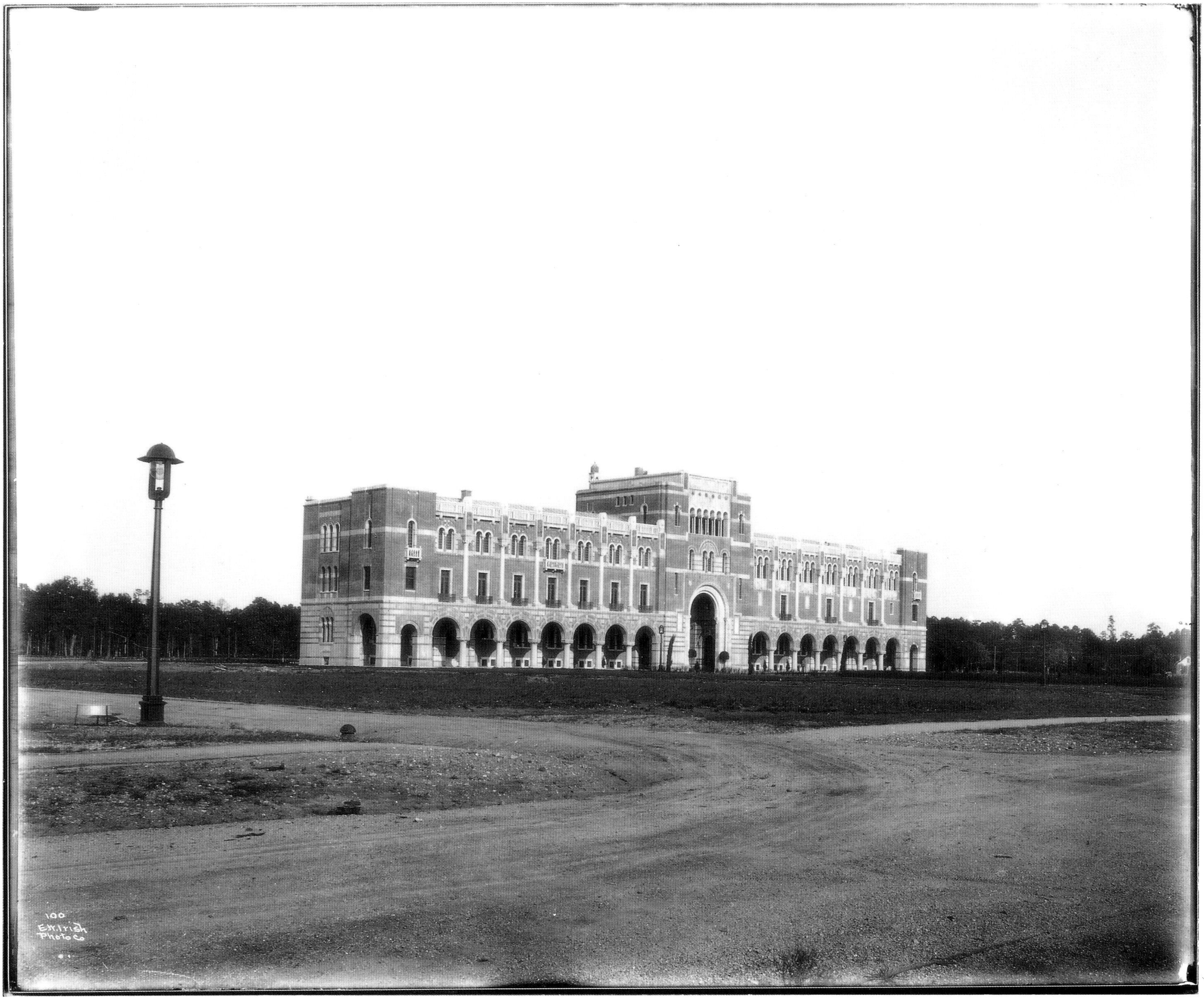
100
E.W.Irish
Photo Co

On September 23, 1900, the elderly William Marsh Rice apparently died in his sleep in his New York City apartment. An alert bank clerk noticed the next day that on a large check signed by Rice and made out to a lawyer the lawyer's name was misspelled; a telephone call for verification revealed that Rice had just died. The bank, sensing that something was wrong, telegraphed Captain Baker in Houston that "Mr. Rice [had] died last night under very suspicious circumstances." Baker immediately set out for New York; meanwhile, the lawyer, Albert T. Patrick, in an interview revealed that Rice had drawn up a new will on June 30, 1900, naming Patrick as legatee, with a subsequent assignment just two days before Rice's death of all the property to Patrick—leaving the Institute nothing. Because these actions did not seem typical of Rice, Captain Baker began an investigation of the suspicious death.

The case created a sensation in New York, especially after Rice's valet, Charles Jones, admitted that he and Patrick had practiced signing Rice's signature, forged the new will, and chloroformed Rice to death after a steady diet of mercury pills had failed to kill the aging millionaire. The elaborate scheme had been undone by a careless slip of the pen. Because he provided state's evidence, Jones was never imprisoned, but mastermind Patrick was convicted and sent to jail until 1912—the date of the opening of the new Institute—when the governor of New York pardoned him. After a disputed will by the second Mrs. Rice was settled in 1904, the Rice Institute finally received a founding endowment of $4.6 million, the first major act of philanthropy to benefit an institution in Texas.

The six trustees now faced the daunting task of turning the paper Institute into a reality. For several years they studied other universities and traveled to the East Coast to inspect a variety of institutions, trying to get an inspired idea of what might be accomplished in Houston. To head the Institute, they chose a person recommended by Woodrow Wilson, president of Princeton. Edgar Odell Lovett, a young, classically educated mathematician teaching at Princeton, formally accepted the offer to be the president of Rice Institute on January 18, 1908. His confidence both in the trustees and in himself had led him to write informally earlier in the month, "I believe we are going to have the patience and the power to do the thing right. . . ."

By the time Lovett arrived in Houston in March, he had already begun to formulate ideas about the Institute he hoped would open in 1910. He wanted to herald its opening with elaborate ceremonies attracting distinguished scholars from around the globe, for this was to be not a small, provincial college or a narrow technical institute but a doctorate-granting university of world stature. A university so conceived must be planned carefully if its high purpose was to be achieved, especially since it was located in a relatively unknown Texas city a thousand miles from other emerging centers of learning like Stanford University and the University of Chicago. The Institute trustees agreed to send Lovett on a nine-month journey in 1908 and 1909 to inspect the leading academic institutions of England, across the Continent, and all the way to Japan; everywhere Lovett interviewed educators, sought nominations for prospective faculty, toured university facilities, and piqued the world's curiosity about the exciting new institution being planned. When Lovett returned to Houston in May 1909, his vision for the Rice Institute was complete, and within the next few months he and the trustees made a series of decisions that would shape its future for a half century.

First, the Institute would be operated solely on the income of the endowment; the principal would not be touched even for buildings. Second, and most boldly, the new institution, although necessarily small at first, aimed not to be merely a trade school or a regional college; instead, it aspired—as Lovett spelled out at the opening ceremonies—"to university standing of the highest grade." Third, since even Rice's handsome endowment was not enough to build a full-fledged university from scratch, it was determined to begin "at the science end," in part at least because science and engineering seemed more applicable to the kinds of "problems pressing for resolution" in "a new and rapidly developing country." Lovett and the trustees intended this limitation to be only temporary.

Southeast façade, Administration Building, 1912

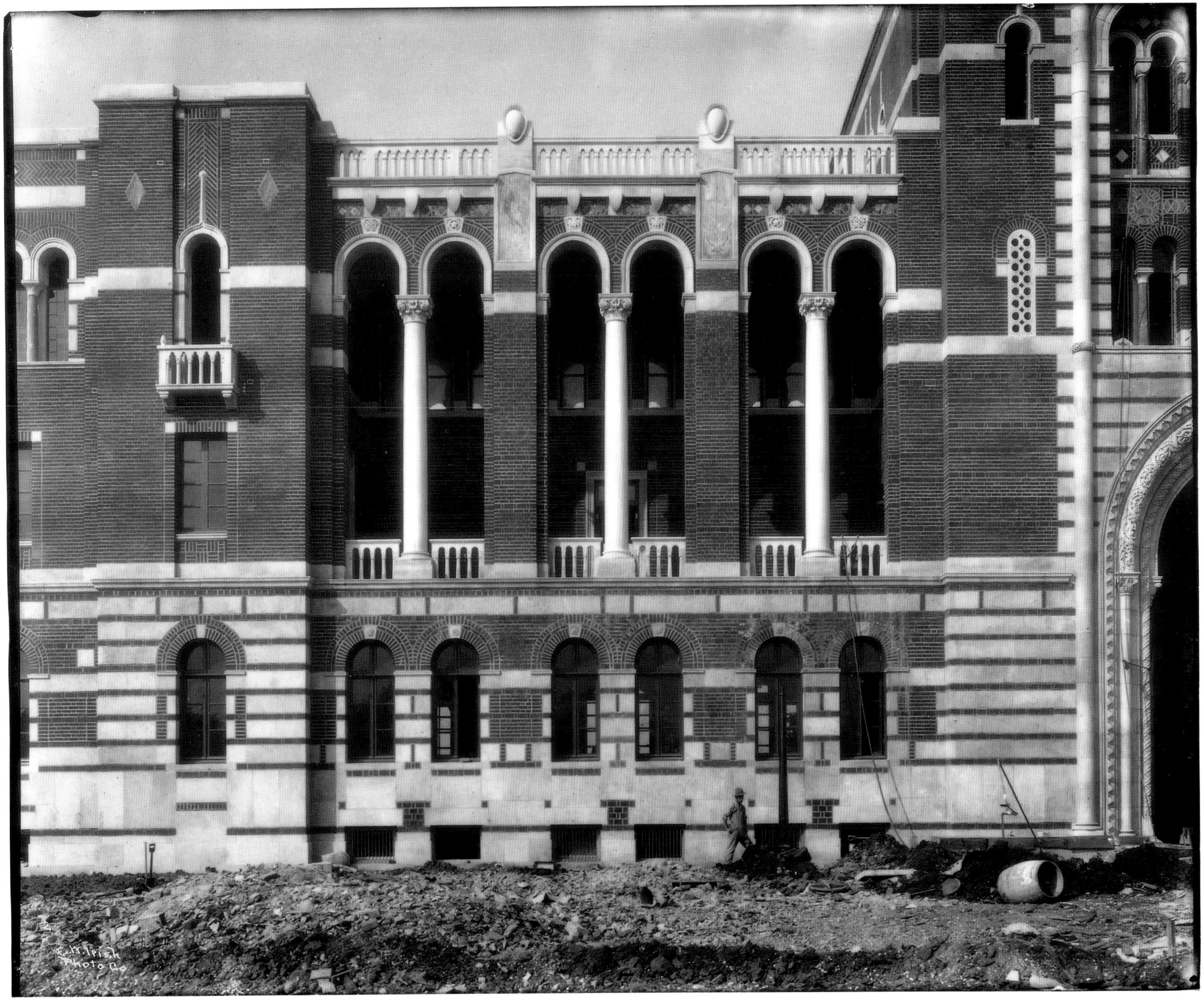
E.H. Irish
Photo Co

Great care was taken in choosing an architect. The trustees selected Ralph Adams Cram of the famed Boston firm of Cram, Goodhue and Ferguson in 1909. Cram accepted the charge very seriously, though he was nonplussed both by the bareness of the prairie campus and by the absence of stylistic precedents in the new country. What should be done? Cram wrote that the firm wanted something that was "beautiful, . . . Southern in its spirit, and with some quality of continuity with the historic and cultural past." The solution was the invention of "something approaching a new style" consisting of elements eclectically chosen from a variety of Mediterranean regions. For this flat, sun-bleached location they wanted to use, Cram wrote, "all the color we could command. A special rose-hued brick, . . . a wonderful rose-and-dove-coloured marble, . . . red Texas granite, . . . glazed, iridescent tiles, green bronze—everything we could think of to give richness, variety, and a certain splendour of effect." Along with the ornate central academic building, whose cornerstone was laid March 2, 1911, and an attached science laboratory, designs for a less detailed engineering laboratory and power plant and the first residence halls were drawn. The smokestack of the power plant was hidden within an elegant brick tower, and this campanile was later to give its name to the Rice yearbook. Grandiose plans for the siting of future buildings, ranked in a series of quadrangles, were finally approved. The original architectural concept has guided the construction of the Rice campus down to the present.

With buildings underway Lovett continued his search for faculty, determined to attract the best scholars he could from the world's leading centers of learning. He had taken to heart what he had been told on his global tour: consider faculty "before mortar and brains before bricks." Lovett's obvious enthusiasm for the educational adventure being launched in Texas helped him attract an international faculty of great distinction. For biology there was Julian Huxley (who returned to England during World War I and later became world famous for his research in developmental biology; he was also a founder of, and first director-general of, UNESCO); for physics there was Harold A. Wilson, FRS, from the Cavendish Laboratory of Cambridge; Thomas Lindsey Blayney with his doctorate from Heidelberg came to teach German; Griffith C. Evans left Harvard to come and teach mathematics (much later a building at Berkeley would be named after him). Within three years others of like prominence joined the faculty: Albert L. Guérard from Stanford to head the French Department; Stockton Axson from Princeton to head English; Harry Boyer Weiser in chemistry; Radoslav A. Tsanoff in philosophy; Hermann J. Muller in biology (after leaving Rice, he won the Nobel Prize in medicine for his work in genetics).

Lovett and the trustees must have been as thrilled by the occasion of the opening of the new university as the first fifty-nine students were who enrolled on September 23, 1912, and gathered with the faculty to hear Lovett's matriculation address. Who would have dared dream of such a confluence of bricks and brains a scant decade before? Yet Lovett had another elaborate academic festival planned during October of that year, with "a galaxy of outstanding savants" representing famous universities around the world. With these ceremonies Lovett was proclaiming to the world the kind of institution Rice was intended ultimately to become, a university international in reputation and influence. Julian Huxley a few years afterward recalled the exhilaration he had experienced at the opening ceremonies. After traveling several miles of almost impassable road from downtown Houston, one was suddenly "confronted by an extraordinary spectacle. . . . The Administration Building was before us, looking almost exactly as if it had risen miraculously out of the earth. . . . [I]t seemed as new and real as a new species of Bird-of-Paradise lit on in a New Guinea jungle. Here it stood, brilliant, astounding, enduring. . . ." That very same impression is made, seventy-five years later, on every visitor who comes upon Lovett Hall at the end of the entrance allée of live oaks.

Approach to the Administration Building from Main Street, 1912

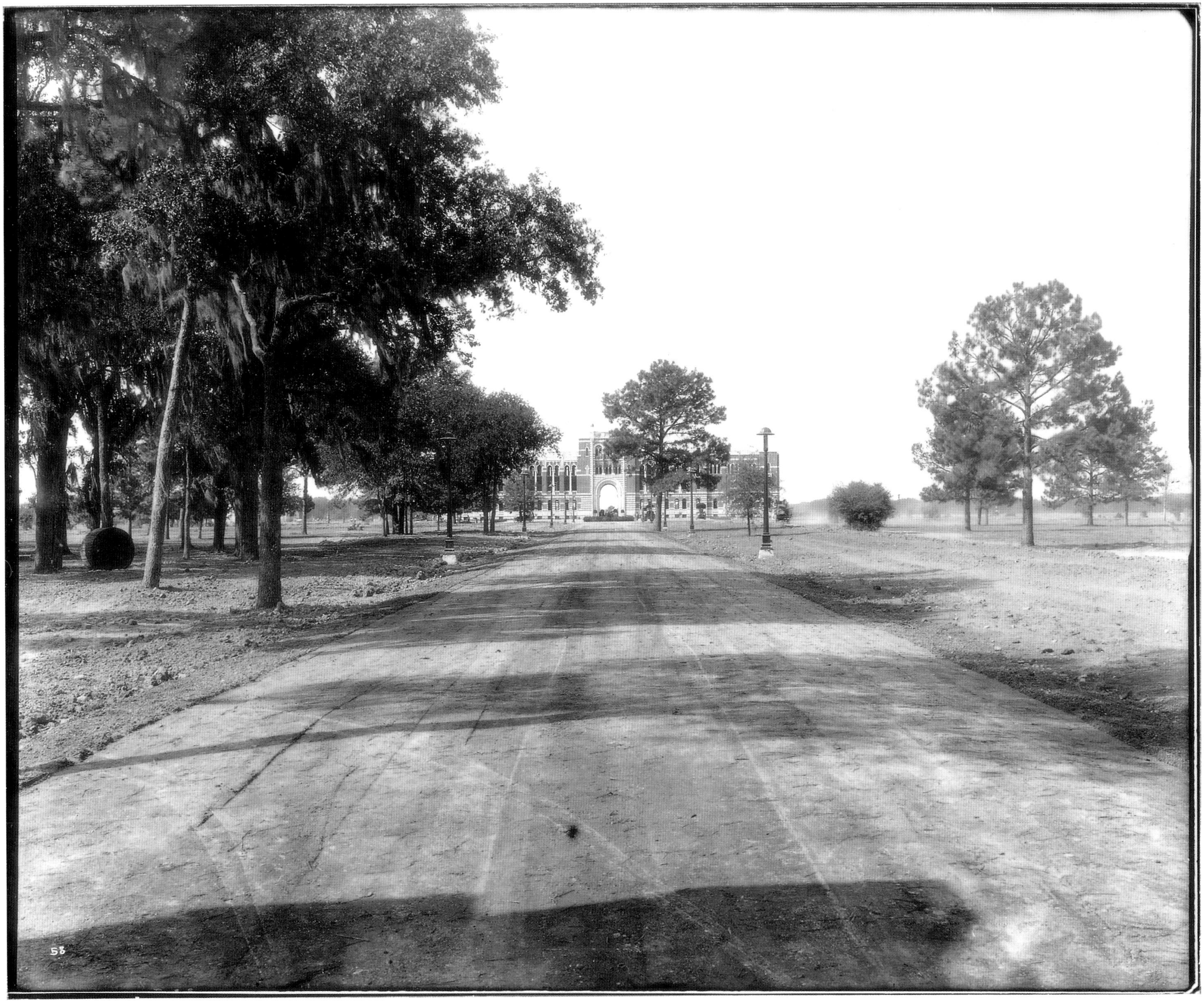
58

Lovett's aspiration for the new institution was breathtakingly bold. "For the present," he wrote, "it is proposed to assign no upper limit to its educational endeavor." He planned on limiting the enrollment—keeping "the standards up and the numbers down" were his words—and maintaining a balance between undergraduate and graduate students. In fact, the interaction between graduate students and undergraduates was deemed particularly beneficial to the undergraduates. The students would be largely self-governed by an honor system, and Lovett announced at the opening ceremonies that "the residential college idea is . . . prominent . . . in the plans of the new institution." He imagined students and faculty as a community of scholars, intermingling in dining halls and common areas, their minds exercised by spirited conversation and their bodies invigorated by intramural sports. Perhaps the spirit of the university was best captured by the inscription on the cornerstone of the first residential hall (now Will Rice College): "To the freedom of sound learning and the fellowship of youth."

The first two decades of academic life at Rice consisted of striving to make real these noble ideals. Several new buildings were added (Physics in 1914, the first field house in 1921, the Chemistry Building in 1925, Cohen House, the faculty club, in 1927), and the character of student life was established. Rice became a charter member of the Southwest Conference in athletics in 1914, and in 1916 students began publishing the student newspaper, *The Rice Thresher,* and the yearbook, *The Campanile*. A school mascot, the owl, and school colors of blue and grey were chosen. Women students lived off-campus at nearby approved boardinghouses (if they did not live with their parents). Students of both sexes quickly identified "underneath the Sallyport" of the administration building as the place to see and be seen. When Autry House (under Episcopal auspices) opened in 1921 on Main Street across from the Institute, it immediately became the unofficial student center, offering meals, facilities for plays and musicals, and a fireside where town students and dorm dwellers alike could meet. Fraternities and sororities were not allowed, but several "literary societies" for women evolved, and they played an important and changing role for more than a half century. High academic standards were the first rule for classwork; Lovett soon arranged for a variety of prizes to be awarded for scholarship. The initial doctorate was awarded in 1918 to Hubert E. Bray in mathematics. Ten years later Rice was accepted as a chapter of Phi Beta Kappa.

Enrollment grew rapidly and soon strained the capacity of the existing facilities. By the early 1920s, with the student population pushing 1,300, it became necessary to limit enrollment. Thereafter, even with higher entrance requirements, applicants still outnumbered available openings. The faculty too grew rapidly and by 1927 numbered seventy in all ranks. Many of the professors beloved by older alumni came during these years. While no partial list could avoid omitting some favorites, during the period from 1920 to 1940 the campus was graced by such scholars as Floyd S. Lear, Lynn M. Case, and David M. Potter in history; Alan D. McKillop and George Williams in English; Marcel Moraud, André Bourgeois, Fred Shelton, and Max Freund in languages; Arthur J. Hartsook and Lewis B. Ryon in engineering; Edgar Altenburg and Asa C. Chandler in biology; Tom Bonner in physics; Floyd E. Ulrich in mathematics; George Holmes Richter in chemistry. John W. Heisman served briefly and unsuccessfully as football coach in the mid-twenties. The faculty did not enjoy tenure, although it was tacitly assumed they would maintain their positions so long as they taught and pursued research at least moderately well. There was only a handful of administrators: Lovett and three trusted associates, John T. McCants, Samuel G. McCann, and William Ward Watkin, ran the entire operation, and there were no departmental secretaries. The Institute was administered with a minimum of rules.

View to the east toward the main gate, 1912

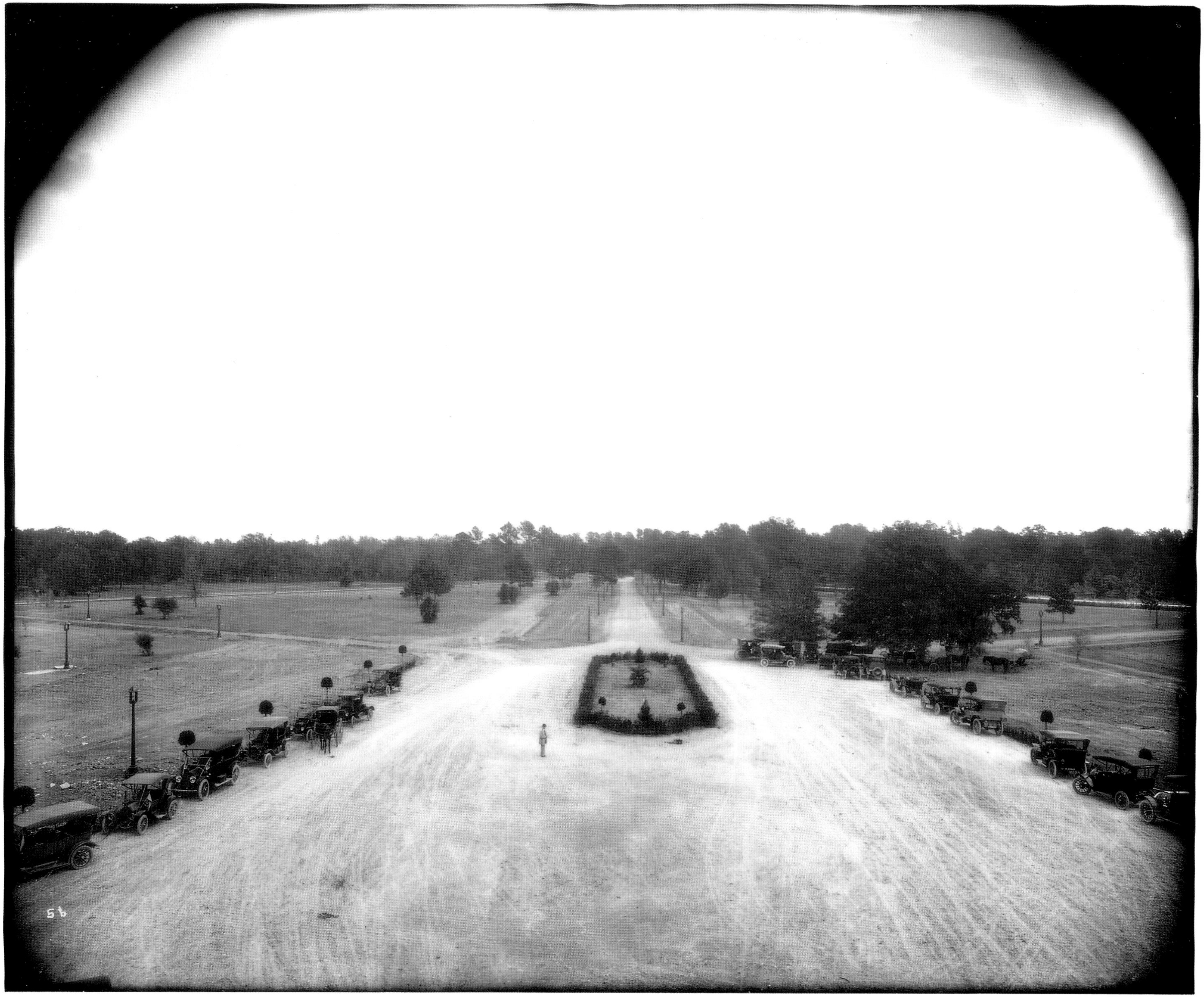

On June 8, 1930, the statue of William Marsh Rice, sculpted by John Angel, was dedicated at its site in the center of the main academic quadrangle, with the ashes of the founder interred at the base of the statue's pedestal. Ironically, though the founder's gift had been munificent in 1904, the trustees had proved to be such cautious money managers that they had hesitated to commit the funds aggressively enough to generate substantial new income. The Institute's endowment, which by 1913 had grown to $10 million, inched up to $12 million in 1923, grew another million by 1933, and by 1943 stood at only $17 million. Moreover, there was a genteel reluctance to ask for donations, and potential donors mistakenly assumed that "wealthy" Rice had no financial needs. Consequently, by the early 1920s, in an era of inflation, Lovett found his dreams for Rice thwarted by a shortage of funds.

Depression-era austerity halted Rice's catapult toward greatness that Lovett had projected in its formative years. Between the two world wars Rice remained primarily a small, undergraduate college for mostly Texas-born students. While this period of quietude was not the destiny Lovett and the trustees had planned in 1912, Rice *was* an excellent college that set academic standards other institutions in the region envied. Rice gained a special place of affection in the hearts of its alumni of those years. Writer John Graves, who attended Rice at the very end of the era, reminisced about life at the Institute then, when students had "a feeling of separateness from time. That," he wrote, "and a sense of study as a way of life, a fusion of living and thinking . . . still seems to me as good a thing as a school can give." He described an English class on Chaucer with Professor Alan McKillop: "In the court below the windows of the room . . . hedges of cape jasmine were in bloom, and the warm drowsy afternoon breeze drove their odor through our brains as we sat for three hours, reading in our turns from *Troilus and Criseyde* or listening while the professorial bass moved regularly along the ancient pentameters. . . . By rights, it should have been impossible to pay any attention at all to sweet Geoffrey. And yet I think it was the most meaningful class I ever sat in. It had a quality of revery. . . . It was Rice as I knew Rice, that class, a summing up."

That "sleepier Rice where the jasmine bloomed," as Graves called it, came to an end in the 1940s. Changes in leadership and the availability of more money in the late 1940s made possible a return to the vision of 1912, and for the next quarter century the campus seemed constantly astir with the construction of buildings and the renewal of academic momentum. On May 14, 1941, the seventy-year-old Lovett offered his resignation after having served as president since 1908. He agreed to continue in office until a successor could be found. The intervening Second World War delayed finding a suitable successor until the last day of 1945, when an eminent physicist from Cal Tech, William Vermillion Houston, was chosen.

In 1942 a fortuitous combination of events had enabled the Institute to become a partial owner of a major oil field in the Rio Grande valley, an investment of incalculable importance that by 1978 had netted the university some $35 million. Two years later trustee chairman Will Rice, as he was called, also died, and was succeeded by Harry C. Wiess, the president of Humble Oil and Refining Company. At Wiess's direction the trustees in early 1945 undertook a careful study of Rice's past and a consideration of its future, spelling out a series of optimistic ten-year goals made feasible by the strengthened financial health of the Institute. It was decided to broaden the curriculum (though still emphasizing science and engineering), expand and diversify graduate work, raise the salaries and increase the number of faculty, seek outside funds in support of the Institute, and enter a major construction program to house the expanded research functions of the university. These ambitious plans marked a return to the goals for the Institute set forth by Lovett in 1912 and resulted in the "metamorphosis" of Rice from the Texas college of the 1930s to the emerging research university of the 1950s, culminating in the significant change of the name in 1960 from The Rice Institute to Rice University.

View from the Administration Building to the west, 1912

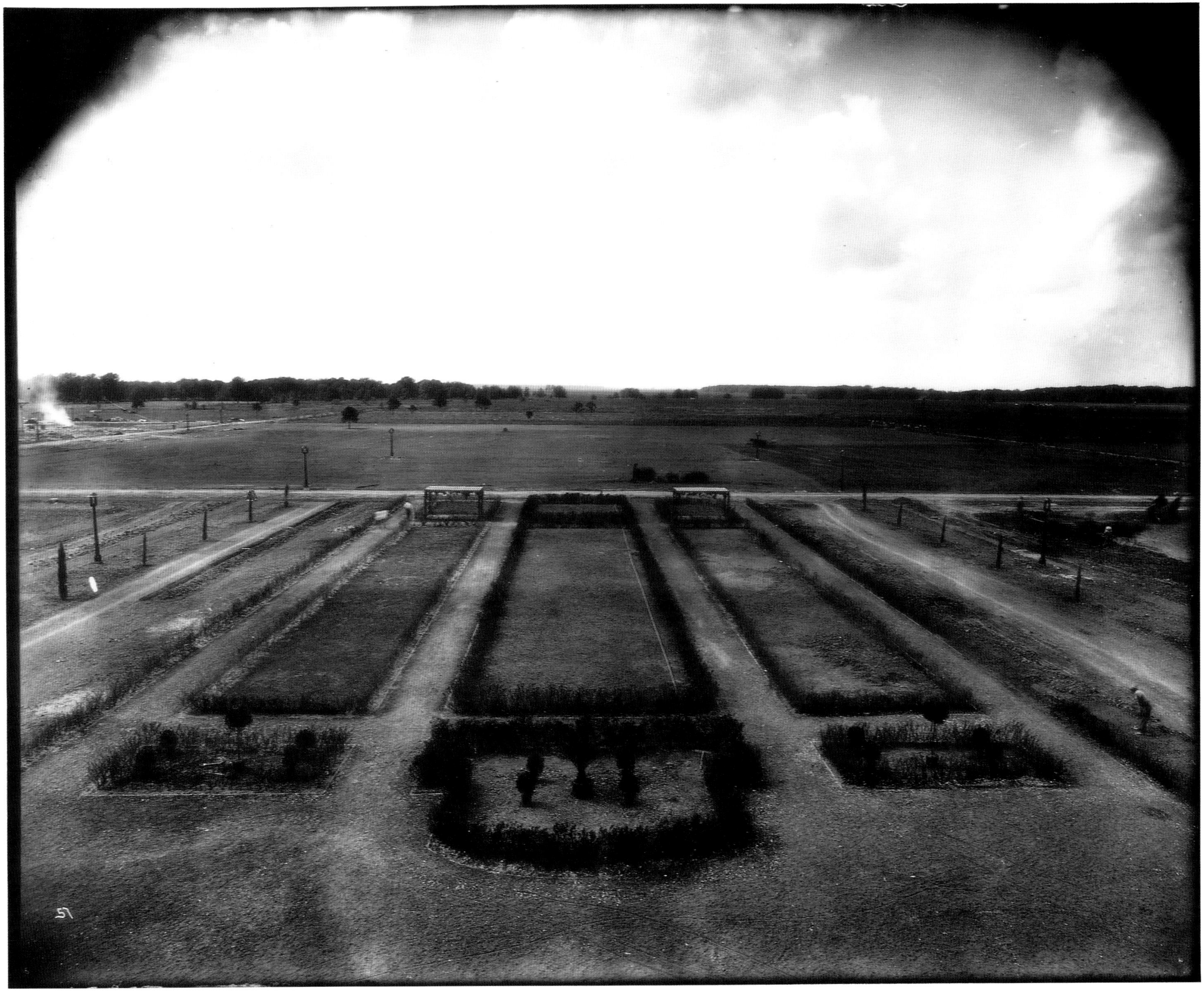

A surge of new construction began to transform the campus. The last academic building had been erected in 1925. Students in 1947 could still stand under the Sallyport and look westward across the open campus and watch the sun set on the horizon. John Graves remembered walking on "the grassy prairie wilderness, with its domed thickets of wild rose, that stretched across the western campus," beyond the measured hedges of the central academic quadrangle. In 1949 Fondren Library closed the western end of the still incomplete academic quadrangle. Adjacent to Fondren was Anderson Hall (1949), with classrooms and faculty offices. A year earlier the engineering laboratory made possible by the Abercrombie family had opened. Additional residential quarters for male students were completed in 1949; Wiess Hall later became Wiess College. A president's house was also built in 1949; a new gymnasium was begun (Autry Court was finished in 1951), and a magnificent football stadium seating 72,000 was built in a frenzied eight months of round-the-clock construction so that it would open in time for the fall schedule in 1950. The huge, paved stadium parking lot ended forever the wild-rose wilderness on the western edge of the campus. Perhaps the expanse of asphalt for stadium parking more than any other campus development signaled the end of the small-time Rice of the pre–World War II days. Big-time academic plans created a new Rice for the postwar atomic age, punctuated in 1952 by the exclamation mark of the tall, windowless tower that housed the nuclear research laboratories.

Changes less visible than buildings were also transforming the character of Rice. Efforts were made to attract more and better-qualified student applicants and to evaluate them more carefully. The undergraduate curriculum was revised in 1947 to assure a broader training for students. For the first time they chose a major; the main courses of study were divided into "academic" (humanities, social science, architecture) and science-engineering curricula, with all students ("academs" and "SE's") taking a wide distribution of courses across the disciplines during their first two years, saving specialization for the final two years. Engineering and architecture students spent an additional fifth year after earning their B.A. taking more specialized courses, then received their B.S. in a specific engineering discipline or in architecture.

Under President Houston's leadership, as the faculty expanded in the late 1940s and 1950s, the scope of the graduate program grew accordingly. By 1950 the multiplying endowment had allowed almost a doubling of the faculty. Many of those who were to build Rice's emerging national reputation arrived in the immediate postwar years. The number of graduate students increased to almost 400 by the end of the 1950s, and made up about 20 percent of the total enrollment—the percentage Lovett had suggested in 1912.

A growing faculty and graduate enrollment once again created a demand for more office and laboratory space, a demand met by another significant spurt of construction. In 1958 the M. D. Anderson Biological Laboratories and the Keith-Wiess Geological Laboratories were opened. Their prizewinning, strikingly modern architecture reflected in color, material, and detail the building style set forth by Cram in 1910. The need for an auditorium led in 1958 to the construction of Hamman Hall, to be used for concerts, plays, speeches, and large lecture courses. The same academic year the Rice Memorial Center (called the RMC) was completed. It housed a snack bar called Sammy's, a chapel, a bookstore, a reading room, meeting rooms, and offices for a variety of student services and activities. The board of trustees, led after 1950 by George R. Brown, provided the substantial monies necessary for such extensive construction: between 1953 and 1963 the endowment grew from $44 million to $102 million.

View to the northeast toward the Rice campus from Main Street, 1912

77.
Ehrish
Photo Co

Student life changed following the war, and not all the changes were positive. Admissions requirements went up, with the result that Rice students were ever more talented. (Self-mocking students would later wear T-shirts or sport bumper stickers that proclaimed: "I go to Rice. I must be smart.") Many of the older students returning from the war were more serious about their classwork than an earlier generation had been. The combination of better, more serious students and more research-oriented faculty meant that the academic experience at Rice became extremely rigorous. Carefree days of rambling amid wild-rose bushes and breathing the sweet scent of jasmine seemed from another world as students struggled to pass the infamous Math 100 and indeed the whole gamut of demanding humanities and laboratory science courses all undergraduates had to take. At times it seemed to students that certain faculty equated hard with good, and a standing joke even as late as the early 1960s was that getting an education at Rice was like getting a drink of water at a fire hydrant. There were wonderful courses and inspiring faculty still—persons like Hubert Bray, Claude Heaps, Floyd S. Lear—and for most students who remembered being considered "different" in high school because they were bright and studious, Rice was often an exhilarating four years. But for many of these same students, shocked at having to compete for C's because of grading curves when they had previously made only A's, Rice seemed at times like a grueling survival course. Occasional student suicides suggested that perhaps Rice was simply too hard for the students' good. One took a kind of perverse pride in sticking it out, imagining all the while how easy friends at other colleges must be having it.

Bright, creative students living together under intense pressure produced wild parties and outrageously elaborate pranks. Freshman hazing continued from the prewar days, along with the slime parade of pajama-clad freshmen down South Main Street, and the senior follies were vaudeville-like skits filled with inside campus jokes and double entendres. These were also the years of Rice's greatest football successes under legendary coach Jess Neely. Pep rallies, bonfires, and the Saturday gridiron contests against hated rivals University of Texas and Texas A&M offered time off from study. As with other campuses, a special vocabulary arose, with extremely studious classmates known as "wieners" or "weenies" and the campus grounds-keepers as "gnomes" (pronounced g-nom-ees). Perhaps the greatest football fan of all was head gardener Tony Martino, who exhorted the team to victory in memorable flights of oratory at pep rallies held Friday nights in front of the library after its 10:00 P.M. closing. Especially in the spring massive water balloon fights erupted between students of adjacent residence halls. The administration recognized and accepted these water balloon wars as harmless ways of letting off steam, but it looked less approvingly at students who explored the underground maze of steam tunnels linking the campus buildings. Persistent efforts to prevent such dangerous adventures were in vain; Rice students daringly organized spelunking clubs for tunnel exploration. Today students wear T-shirts displaying a map of the tunnel system, emblazoned with the words "Strictly off limits: tours available."

First class of the Rice Institute with President Edgar O. Lovett (center), 1912

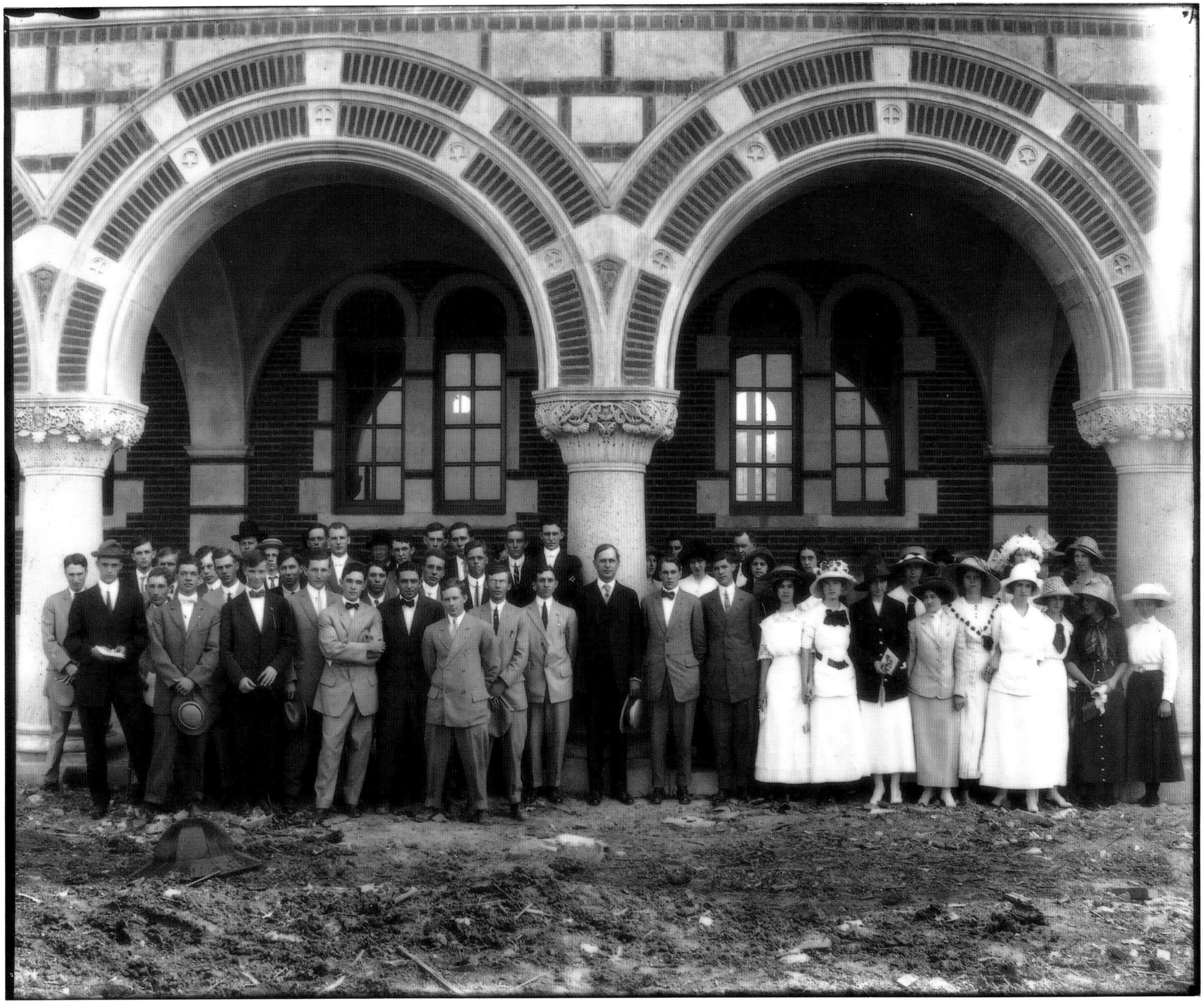

President Lovett had envisioned a democratic residential college system in 1912, but no progress was made until the mid-1950s. There had never been fraternities at Rice, only residence halls for men, although the women's literary societies had acquired a sorority-like social exclusiveness by the late 1940s. Adviser to women Betty Rose Dowden ended this tendency in 1950 by helping to organize enough new literary societies that every woman student could belong to one. Still, women could not live on campus, and the dormitories for men left much to be desired. Recognizing that student life and morale at Rice were not meeting the standards the Institute otherwise aspired to, the trustees decided to make additions to the three older residence halls and the newer Wiess Hall, transforming them into four men's colleges: Baker, Hanszen, Will Rice, and Wiess, named after prominent benefactors (trustees Captain James Baker, Harry Clay Hanszen, nephew-of-the-founder William M. Rice, Jr., and Harry C. Wiess). While these plans were underway, Houston Endowment, Inc., provided funds for a women's college to be named for financier Jesse Jones's wife, Mary Gibbs Jones. Each college was to have its own dining hall, detached master's house, apartments for two or more resident single faculty, study rooms, game rooms, and space for approximately 220 students. The colleges would consist of students representing all classes, freshman to senior, and all majors. Each college would be independently governed by its own student officers, and each would sponsor its own intramural teams, plays, glee clubs, and the like. Fifteen or more nonresident faculty associates would be chosen for each college to take occasional meals there and participate to a degree in the life of that college. The development of the college system, with students moving into the new facilities in the spring of 1957, was the single most dramatic improvement in student life ever made at Rice; it transformed the undergraduate experience.

It was not simply that the facilities represented a vast improvement in the amenities of everyday life—the men's colleges remained unairconditioned, and on warm nights when the wind blew from the south, students could hear lions roaring at the nearby Houston zoo—but the colleges profoundly changed the character of campus life. Women living on campus was a milestone, even though they had strict curfews and dress codes. Men and women studying together in the library before the long walk to Jones College (prudently placed across the campus from the men's colleges) made life more pleasant for many students. The college system rendered student organization by class almost irrelevant, and henceforth students came to identify far more with their college than with their graduation class. Intramural competition became more spirited, and colleges came to be recognized for their glee club or their Shakespearean plays or their table-top theater. The colleges slowly gained an identity, an ethos, that set them apart from one another; upperclassmen became less interested in initiating freshmen by hazing and more interested in incorporating them into the life of the colleges. Freshman week evolved to ease the transition from high school to Rice, with surprisingly supportive involvement from large numbers of upperclassmen. While life in the colleges has not yet achieved the degree of intellectual and social camaraderie idealized by Lovett, it is a far cry from dorm life. Within a decade colleges had become in student eyes the most distinctive (and most praised) characteristic of Rice.

Delegates and visitors to the Opening Ceremonies, 1912

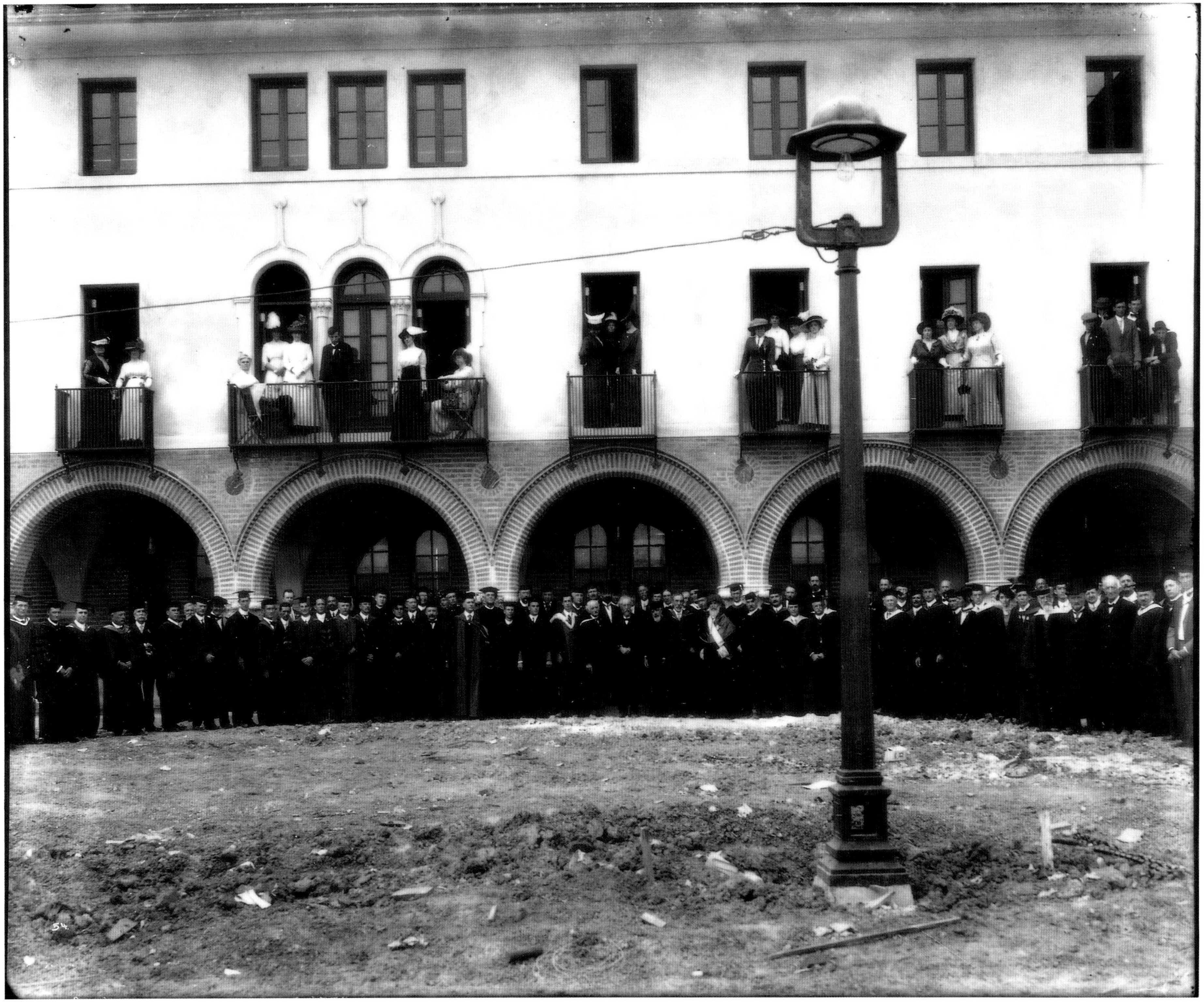

The beer-bike race, perhaps Rice's most colorful athletic event, began in 1957 with the college system. The event is a modified relay race: a rider may leave the starting area only after a "chugger" from his team has drained a 24-ounce can of beer or other warm beverage. In the early years, the same people drank beer and rode bikes, but later drinkers and riders were separate. Originally, too, the race among the four men's colleges ran around the inner loop circling Lovett Hall, the library, and the student center. Later, the event was laid out on the stadium parking lot.

College spirit has always run high; by the 1970s and 1980s the spring beer-bike race had become more important to most students than the homecoming football game in the fall. The colleges today arrange elaborate and comical entrances to the stands. Preceding the main event is a shorter women's beer-bike race, an alumni race, and a whimsical Graduate Student Association race. Younger alumni in growing numbers return to campus for this spring outing, complemented now with tennis matches, baseball games, and free poor boys and other refreshments. Though the athletes are amateurs, the fans are fervent in support of their colleges. The new 21-year-old age limit for alcoholic consumption has forced some adjustments in procedures, but the excitement and good natured competitiveness of the races remain. Beer-bike day has become a quintessentially Rice event.

As the 1950s ended, an important era in Rice's history was ending too, and a new phase of growth and development was about to begin. During the summer of 1957 Edgar Odell Lovett had died, having lived to see the college system established but not to see Rice's name changed to "university" in 1960. In 1947, when the administration building was renamed in his honor, the inscription had read: "He has reared a monument more lasting than brass," and in truth Rice was very much his lengthened shadow. The 1950s brought new construction and ever-increasing faculty (almost 175 by the end of the decade), new academic departments such as geology, and a greater commitment to the humanities and social sciences (for example, the editorial offices on campus of the *Journal of Southern History,* and later the *Papers of Jefferson Davis* and *Studies in English Literature*). Smaller, highly visible changes, too, transformed the campus—the gravel paths became pebble and aggregate sidewalks, and cars could no longer drive through the center of the campus. Obviously Rice was in flux. In the fall of 1960 bad health forced President Houston to resign, and for a few months the charismatic geologist and provost, Carey Croneis, served as acting president. Then at the June 1961 commencement the board of trustees announced the appointment of Rice's third president, chemist Kenneth Sanborn Pitzer of the University of California at Berkeley, where he had been a friend of mathematician and one-time Rice professor Griffith Evans.

Perhaps from Evans President Pitzer learned of the high aspirations Lovett had had for the Rice Institute from the very beginning of its history; certainly Pitzer came to Rice determined to help the university achieve those early ambitions. When Pitzer arrived, Rice was still better known for its undergraduate programs than for its small graduate programs. In the post–World War II era, university reputations were based almost entirely on the strength of their graduate offerings. At the same time modern science-engineering research required teams of professors and graduate students. Pitzer and the board of trustees also recognized the need for a private research university of the first rank in the Southwest. For all these reasons plans were made to improve Rice's stature as a graduate institution. There would be more additions to the campus, the faculty would be increased in size, the graduate enrollment would be doubled (from approximately 400 to 800 students), and all the while the university's one indisputable claim to excellence, its undergraduate programs, would be strengthened. What was intended was to lead Rice past the threshold of being a good regional university to being a good national university. To do so would require administrative leadership and board money, the commitment of the faculty, major new sources of money, and freedom from two inhibiting features of the 1891 charter.

*Opening Ceremonies,
President Lovett addressing the audience, 1912*

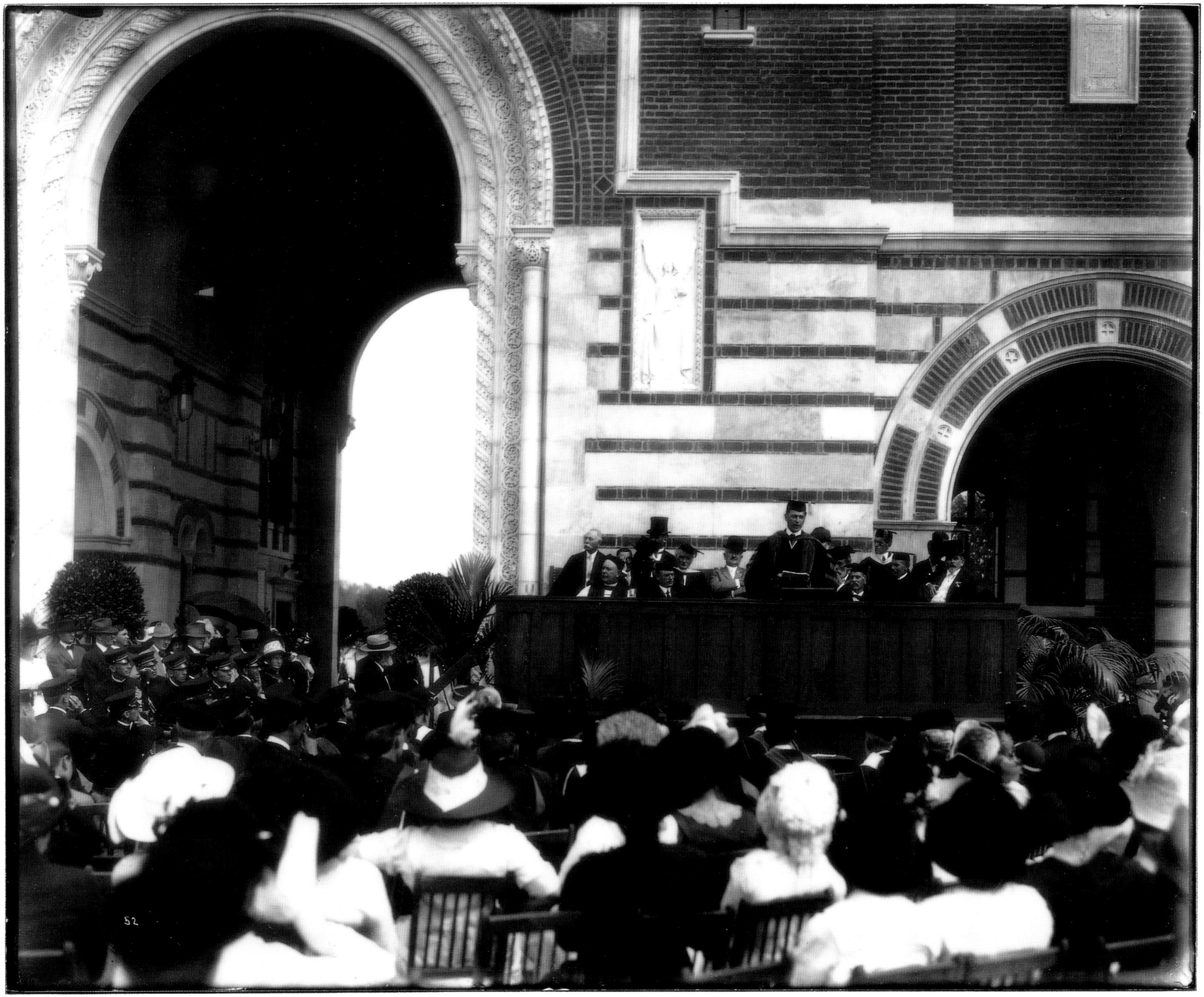
52

Largely because of trustee chairman George Brown's foresight, the endowment had grown rapidly, but additional sources of funds would have to be identified. Many potential donors and foundations still mistakenly believed that Rice, since it did not charge tuition, had an abundance of wealth and did not need contributions. As early as 1941 the trustees had considered petitioning the courts to change the terms of the 1891 charter, but the Rincon oil field purchase had made such a move unnecessary. Now, in the 1960s, if Rice were to realize its plans for expansion, a great deal of new money had to be raised. Consequently the trustees decided in 1962 to bring legal action to make it possible to charge tuition, which was allowed after four years of court debate.

Now half of the revision sought by the trustees was accomplished. In keeping with the spirit of the times in which he lived, William Marsh Rice had specified that Rice was to be open to men and women students who were "white inhabitants of the City of Houston, and State of Texas." While out-of-state students had been accepted from the first, and Asian students had been attending for a generation or more, Pitzer, the trustees, and the faculty recognized in 1962 that no southern university could attain national distinction if it discriminated against black students. Not only was it morally wrong, but such discrimination made it difficult to attract faculty and government research funds. The world had changed dramatically since 1891; William Marsh Rice's primary aim had been to establish an educational institution of the first rank; hence, logic compelled the trustees to join the issue of desegregation with the request to charge tuition, and the conjoined issues were sent to court together.

With the racial stigma and the tuition ban removed, Rice was primed for a significant move upward in the ranks of American higher education. Reminiscent of the late 1940s, there was again an impressive spurt of new construction: Rayzor Hall for the humanities in 1962, Ryon Engineering Building in 1965, the Space Science Building in 1966, Allen Center (the campus business office) in 1967, Herman Brown Hall for mathematics and mathematical sciences in 1968, a major addition to the library also in 1968, the Media Center in 1970. In 1971 Cleveland Sewall Hall for the fine arts and the social sciences was completed. Elaborately detailed to complement Lovett Hall and to mirror the Physics Building, this five-story, academic hall closed the main academic quadrangle. Moreover, to house an expanded undergraduate body eventually approaching 2,600 students, three new colleges were opened—Brown College in 1965, Lovett College in 1968, and Sid Richardson College in 1971.

By the end of the 1960s the faculty had doubled again, now numbering more than 350. In 1962 a long-overdue system of tenure was adopted, making it easier to attract scholars from other universities and setting up a mechanism to evaluate new faculty in terms of clearly understood procedures. New departments such as space science and biochemistry were added and planned, while smaller departments that had been grouped together, such as anthropology, psychology, and sociology, were separated and enlarged. Indeed, by the end of the decade Rice's total enrollment for the first time exceeded 3,000, and the teacher-student ratio fell below 10 to 1.

For many undergraduates these were exciting but trying years. Math 100 still struck terror in their hearts and turned many an aspiring science-engineering student into a chastened academ. Grading at Rice still bordered on the punitive. The grade distribution for all undergraduate courses in the Fall 1961 semester revealed that 63 percent of freshman grades were C or lower; over half the grades in 400-level courses were C or lower. One third of the freshman class did not graduate for academic reasons, even though their average standardized test scores proved that Rice students were among the ablest in the nation. By the end of the decade welcome changes in faculty grade expectations were made. A special freshman math course for academs was devised—*pace* Math 100. Distribution requirements were changed, and much heavier emphasis was placed on excellence in teaching with superior teachers receiving the Brown awards. In the 1960s Rice students were named Rhodes scholars and Marshall scholars, and the 1966 Rice College Bowl Team won the national championship, Rice's only bowl victory in the last quarter century.

Opening Ceremonies, a lecture in the faculty chamber, 1912

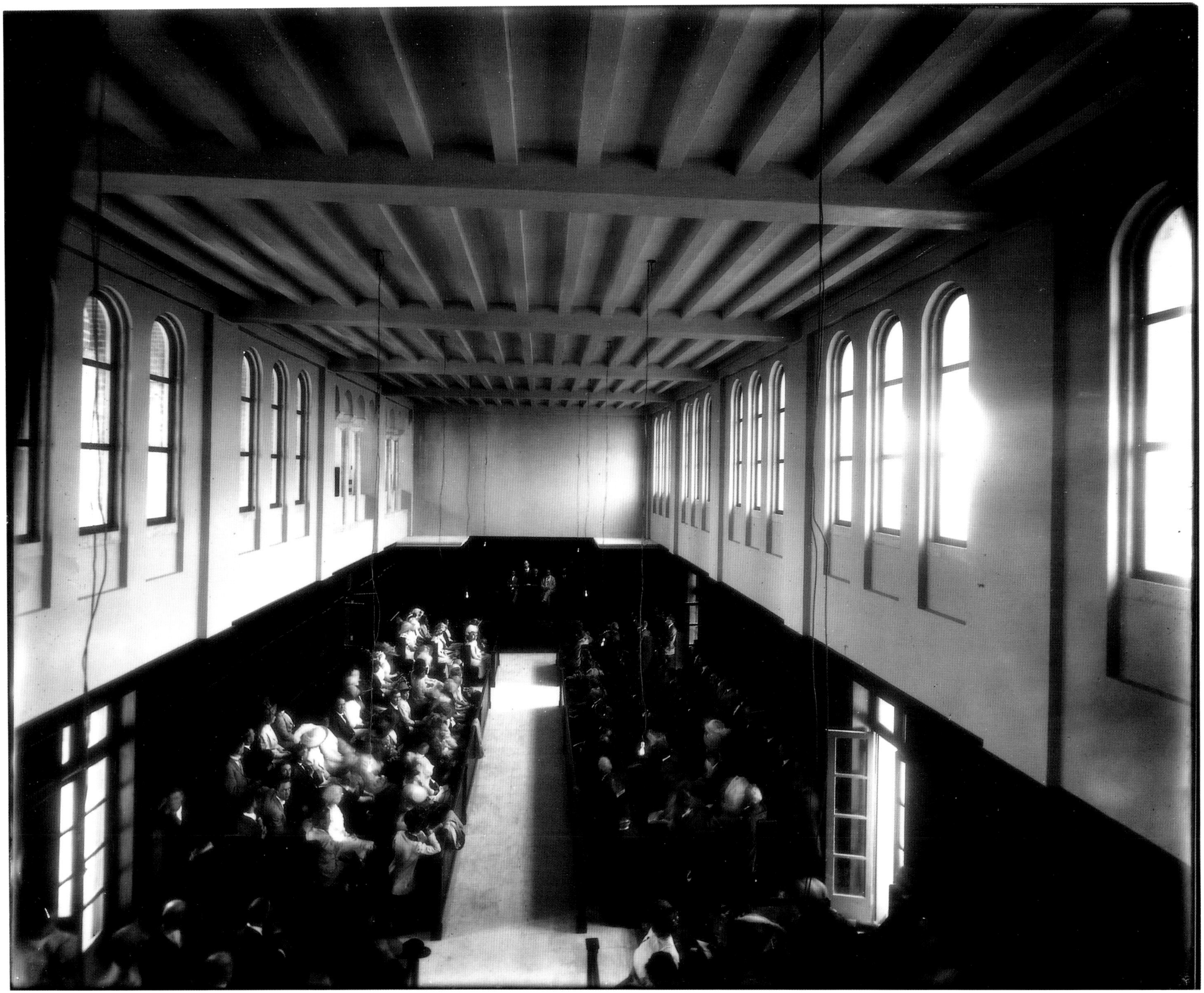

The student generation at Rice—as across the nation—was caught up in the ferment and turmoil of the 1960s. Rock music, the civil rights movement, the Vietnam War and accompanying protests, changing views toward drugs, dress, and sex—American attitudes underwent profound changes in a short span of time. Rice students may have seemed polite and apathetic when compared to media stereotypes of students at Berkeley and Columbia, but, compared to their predecessors in the 1950s, Rice students in the 1960s were concerned, committed, and rebellious. The issues that moved them were the issues that engaged students elsewhere: political injustice, racism, the war in Vietnam. A section of the student center was fire-bombed. Students also began to question aspects of university life and worked toward campus reforms. Dress codes for women were relaxed—they could wear slacks, then jeans, and eventually shorts; visiting hours for the opposite sex in the colleges were liberalized; the curriculum became far more flexible and the grading less harsh. More than ever before, the colleges became the center of student life.

In most ways the student experience at Rice became healthier after the reforms and changed attitudes of the mid-1960s. Students seemed happier with greater freedom in their choice of courses, though faculty worried about whether they chose wisely. Less rigorous grading produced more relaxed, more creative students who were definitely more satisfying to teach. The breadth of cultural activities at the colleges expanded severalfold, with a smorgasbord of plays, after-dinner talks, musical events, and movies to choose from. The bright Rice students proved that they were not "nerds" who only studied. In fact, their skills were only partly academic, and most had other impressive talents. From college cabarets that showcased musical, comedic, and other theatrical abilities to creative parties like Archi-Arts, the School of Architecture's annual ball, and Wiess College's tongue-in-cheek Night of Decadence, Rice was more than simply work. The zany side of Rice students saw new life with the transformation of the Rice Band from a poor-man's version of the big state university bands into the irreverent Marching Owl Band (the MOB), whose outrageous antics and satiric skits at half time made fans forget the lopsided scores.

Rice University paused in October 1962 to celebrate its semicentennial. On the fiftieth anniversary of the opening, another galaxy of internationally distinguished scholars was assembled in an academic festival both to mark what had been accomplished in Houston in five decades and to suggest what remained to be done. Throughout the year a series of symposia provided an ongoing intellectual feast. As in 1912, Rice was making a statement about the place it wished to take in the academic world.

President Pitzer understood that Rice should provide academic leadership in its region of the nation, and he consciously sought to make Rice more like Stanford, recognizing all the while that Rice had certain unique features. In 1968 Pitzer resigned the presidency of Rice to become president of Stanford itself. When the trustees announced in February 1969 their choice for the new president, historian and former dean William H. Masterson, many students and faculty protested, and within several days Masterson withdrew his name. Subsequently history professor Frank E. Vandiver served as acting president for the remainder of 1969 and 1970. After an extensive search, the board of trustees announced Rice's fourth president, chemist Norman Hackerman, then president of the University of Texas at Austin. Hackerman came to a university that had just completed its most expansive twenty-five years, with plans already underway for a significant broadening of its programs. The Institute for the Arts had begun in 1969, and the Shepherd School of Music was being developed, to open in 1974. Both would transform the artistic dimension of life at Rice, with new courses, exhibits, and concerts. The Media Center, with its extensive photography program and film offerings, became a resource for the Rice community and indeed the entire city.

But these welcome developments also presented a dilemma to President Hackerman, for the generation of expansion in programs and personnel had stretched to the limits the financial resources of the university, substantial as the endowment was. The university had run slight deficits in the late 1960s, and President Hackerman's first obligation was to balance programs with means. The result was a decade of consolidation and reining in grandiose plans and making sure new programs were fully endowed before they were begun.

New programs did develop during the 1970s, but President Hackerman was most concerned with restructuring and rationalizing the university's administration. The Office of Advanced Studies and Research was organized in 1972 to coordinate graduate studies and funded research programs. The Division of Science and Engineering was split into two schools in 1975, the appropriately named George R. Brown School of Engineering and the School of Natural Sciences (renamed the Wiess School of Natural Sciences in 1979). Similarly the Division of Humanities and Social Sciences became two separate schools in 1979; these four schools, added to the new music school and the graduate school of administration, and the School of Architecture, which had been organized in 1965, brought the total to seven, each with its own dean. The computer operations were expanded into the Institute for Computer Services and Applications in 1971; twelve years later ICSA (pronounced ik-suh) moved into its own building. Rice's administration was growing in order to address the needs of a larger, more complex, more research-oriented university. Such reorganization became one of the hallmarks of the Hackerman years. "Centers" were founded to coordinate specialized research and services; among the more than dozen centers were the Rice Center for Community Design and Research (1972), the Rice Engineering Design and Development Institute (1978), the Rice Quantum Institute (1980), the Rice Institute for Policy Analysis (1981), and the four-university consortium, the Houston Area Research Center (1982). As Charles Garside, Jr., of Rice's department of history said in April 1985 at a special faculty convocation honoring President Hackerman upon his retirement, this administrative restructuring "restored equilibrium" to the university and connected Hackerman's term philosophically to that of Lovett in their common desire to promote liberal and technical learning.

Another hallmark of the Hackerman years was providing for the long-range financial needs of the university. President Lovett had been forced to defer his dreams of Rice's quick escalation into the top tier of universities by the economic exigencies of the post-World War I years and the Depression years. President Hackerman, in Garside's words, "found himself confronted by a concern for the financial security of the University not unlike that of President Lovett. With an unanticipated vigor and single-mindedness he addressed himself to the problem immediately." The development office began in earnest in 1970, and within fifteen years it had raised more than $200 million. In 1976 the Brown Foundation, in one of the most significant decisions ever made on behalf of the university, extended to Rice a ten-year, $20 million challenge grant to inspire the university and its friends to generate new levels of support. In 1982 this challenge was renewed for another ten years, bringing the total of Brown Foundation gifts during the projected period to more than $50 million; at the same time the Brown matching money attracted additional tens of millions of dollars. This Brown Foundation challenge represents one of the largest gifts to a single academic institution in the history of American higher education. Such contributions, combined with President Hackerman's stewardship of the total university resources, resulted in a dramatic growth in the endowment, which climbed from $131 million in 1970 to $484 million in 1984. These figures speak for themselves. They allow Rice to provide deserving students an outstanding education at a tuition cost less than half that of comparable institutions, with generous scholarship support that guarantees that any deserving student admitted can afford to attend.

The campus experienced little construction during the 1970s. Nevertheless, these were active, rewarding years at Rice. The library, which had owned sixty-nine books in 1912, passed the one-million-volume mark in 1979 and began to bulge at the seams. In 1980 the Woodson Research Center of the library acquired the papers of its first biology professor, Sir Julian Huxley. Robert W. Wilson in 1978 became the first Rice alumnus to win a Nobel Prize (in 1986 Larry McMurtry would win the Pulitzer Prize for his novel, *Lonesome Dove*). Baker and Hanszen colleges in 1973 were made coeducational; within a decade all but two of the colleges had become coed, to the great delight of the students. Rice had come a long way since the years when women were not allowed on campus after 5:00 P.M.

The Office of Continuing Studies was begun in 1972, and at first most of its offerings were of a technical nature. Soon it branched out into a variety of areas, from its novel "Living Texas" program, which explained to Houston newcomers unusual aspects of the life and culture of the Lone Star State, to a long list of noncredit courses on such topics as art, history, literature, photography, crafts, and computers. An innovative publishing program brought experts in publishing to the campus to offer a summer institute on how to plan, design, market, edit, and publish books and periodicals. At times in the past Rice had been considered aloof from the community, but now thousands of alumni and community people were attracted to the campus for the special courses. The Mellon Foundation also underwrote in the schools of social sciences and humanities a series of two-week summer seminars for teachers in small colleges in Texas and contiguous states.

Suddenly in the early 1980s, after a ten-year hiatus in construction, more buildings and additions were begun. Abercrombie Laboratories were renovated and enlarged. Anderson Hall acquired an elegant wing designed by the British architect James Stirling. The Seeley G. Mudd Computer Science Building was completed in 1983 and Herring Hall for the Jones School in 1984. A new building for materials science, underwritten by John L. Cox, completed the Engineering Quadrangle in 1984, with the quadrangle itself strikingly complemented by the installation in December 1984 of three massive granite monoliths, conceived and displayed by sculptor Michael Heizer and dedicated to Rice's major donor, George R. Brown. A handsome addition to the Rice Memorial Center, also designed by Cesar Pelli, was begun in 1984 and named in honor of the Ley family, who contributed substantially to it.

When in March 1984 President Hackerman announced his imminent retirement, he could well take comfort in the health of the institution. Clearly Rice had been brought to the very threshold of the kind of greatness envisioned at its founding. Houston was no longer a small southern marketing center—the Magnolia City, it called itself in 1912—but a large, dynamic, cosmopolitan city with enormous cultural, medical, scientific, and economic resources. The university's 3,800 students were among the most able on any American campus, whether measured by average SAT scores, the number of National Merit Scholarship winners, or by the percentage of graduates who had earned a doctorate (Rice ranked sixteenth overall in the nation). A faculty of more than 400 included scholars and artists of international distinction. The endowment of the university was the envy of other universities everywhere. Rice's future seemed bright indeed.

Residential halls, 1912

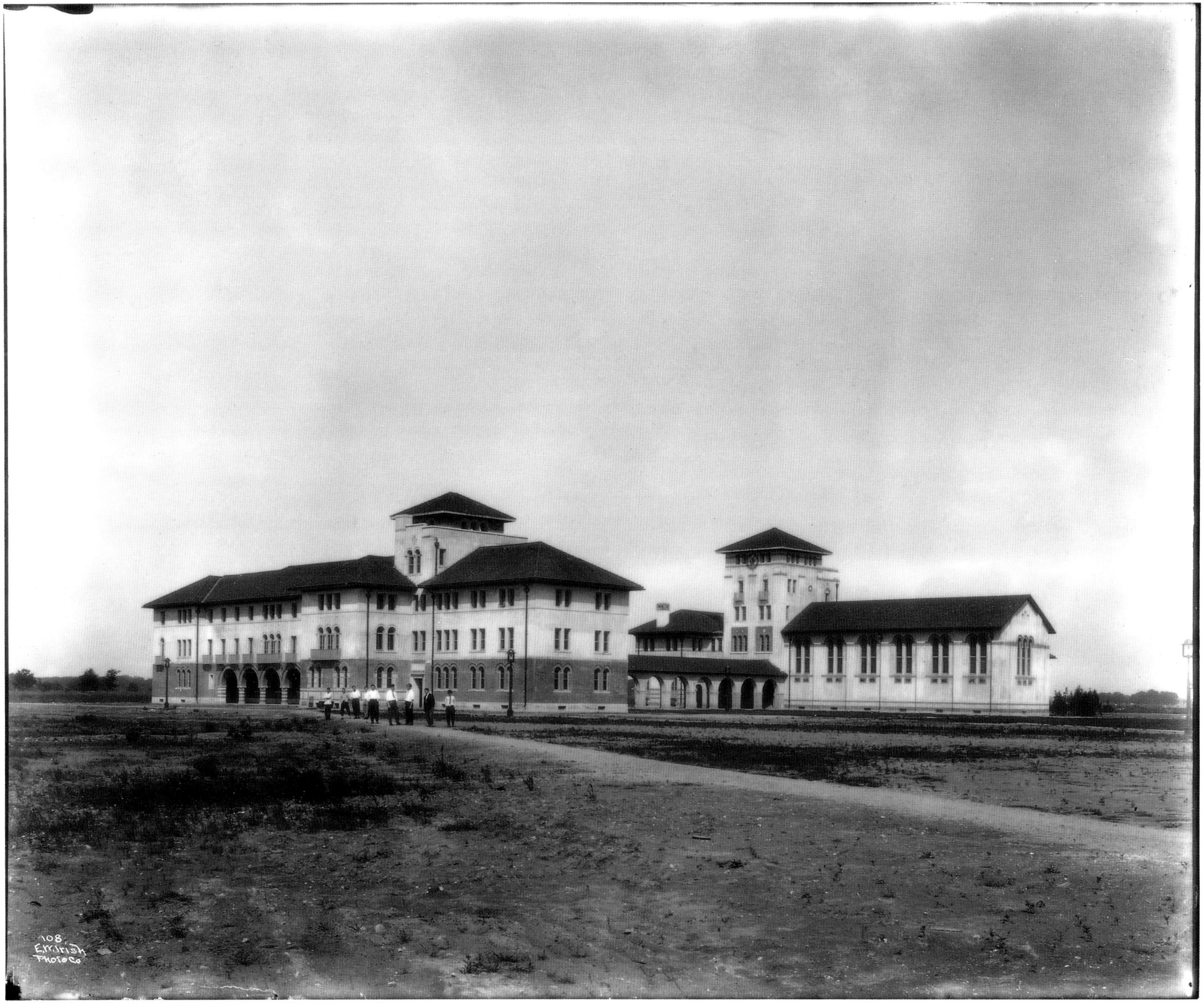
108.
E.M.Irish
Photo Co

It was just that potential that attracted theologian George E. Rupp, dean of the Harvard Divinity School, to become Rice's fifth president. Those few who still considered Rice a science-engineering institute were surprised by the choice of a humanist, but the trustees' choice reflected Rice's maturation into a complete university. As President Rupp and his family moved to Houston in the summer of 1985, Rice was admitted to the ranks of the Association of American Universities.

The pomp and pageantry of George Rupp's inaugural ceremony on October 25, 1985, brightened an otherwise cloudy day, and the rain clouds restrained themselves just long enough for the audience of students, alumni, friends, faculty, and distinguished visitors to hear President Rupp's inaugural commitment "to stand with Edgar Odell Lovett" in insisting on three proud traditions at Rice. "First, we will continue to offer outstanding education to the most capable students we can attract, irrespective of their ability to pay." And their education will help bridge the chasm between what C. P. Snow has called the two cultures of science and the humanities, for Rice since the beginning has been and will remain dedicated to "liberal and technical learning." Second, Rupp emphasized, "we will continue and intensify our efforts in research, scholarship, and professional accomplishment." Rice has always stood for the expansion of knowledge as well as its communication, and that tradition will be honored. Third, President Rupp pledged "to uphold and extend . . . the very conception of education that animated the founder of this institution . . . service to the broader society." He pointed out how fortunate the Rice community of scholars was to be able to work on such a beautiful campus, and he emphasized the opportunities for interdisciplinary study and cooperation that Rice's small scale afforded.

Within a year President Rupp began to project his plans for enhancing the university. The undergraduate experience was to continue to receive emphasis. Accordingly the curriculum would be reviewed to see if it could be improved. At the same time, the graduate programs were to be strengthened by building on areas of existing excellence. While overall the present graduate program lacks the distinction of the undergraduate, there are pockets of great strength. Because the nation's outstanding graduate departments are two to twenty times larger than corresponding departments at Rice, there is no way across-the-board graduate strength can be achieved at Rice without changing the fundamental nature of the university, and that would clearly be undesirable. However, by carefully choosing "targets of opportunity," five clusters of research activity of high quality ranging across a variety of departments have been initially identified. Approximately ten new faculty members with interdisciplinary interests and great distinction or promise will be named to departments participating in the five institutes. These new scholars will broaden the offerings of the separate departments and, through their interaction with other researchers in the cluster areas chosen for enhancement, will provide the critical mass of faculty necessary for graduate programs of indisputable international prominence. It is further proposed that a building program be commenced to provide "unsurpassed facilities"—planned at first are a major complex for the Shepherd School of Music and a state-of-the-art science laboratory. A significant and long-needed renovation of the first-floor, public areas of Fondren Library is also underway, with other projects in the discussion stage. The first five enhancement clusters are to be the Rice Quantum Institute, the Biosciences/Bioengineering Institute, the Institute of Computer and Information Technology, the Center for Institutions and Values, and the Center for Cultural Studies. In those research areas Rice "has the potential," according to Rupp, "to be as good as any place in the world" without losing the advantages of its small size.

Residential hall, interior commons room, 1912

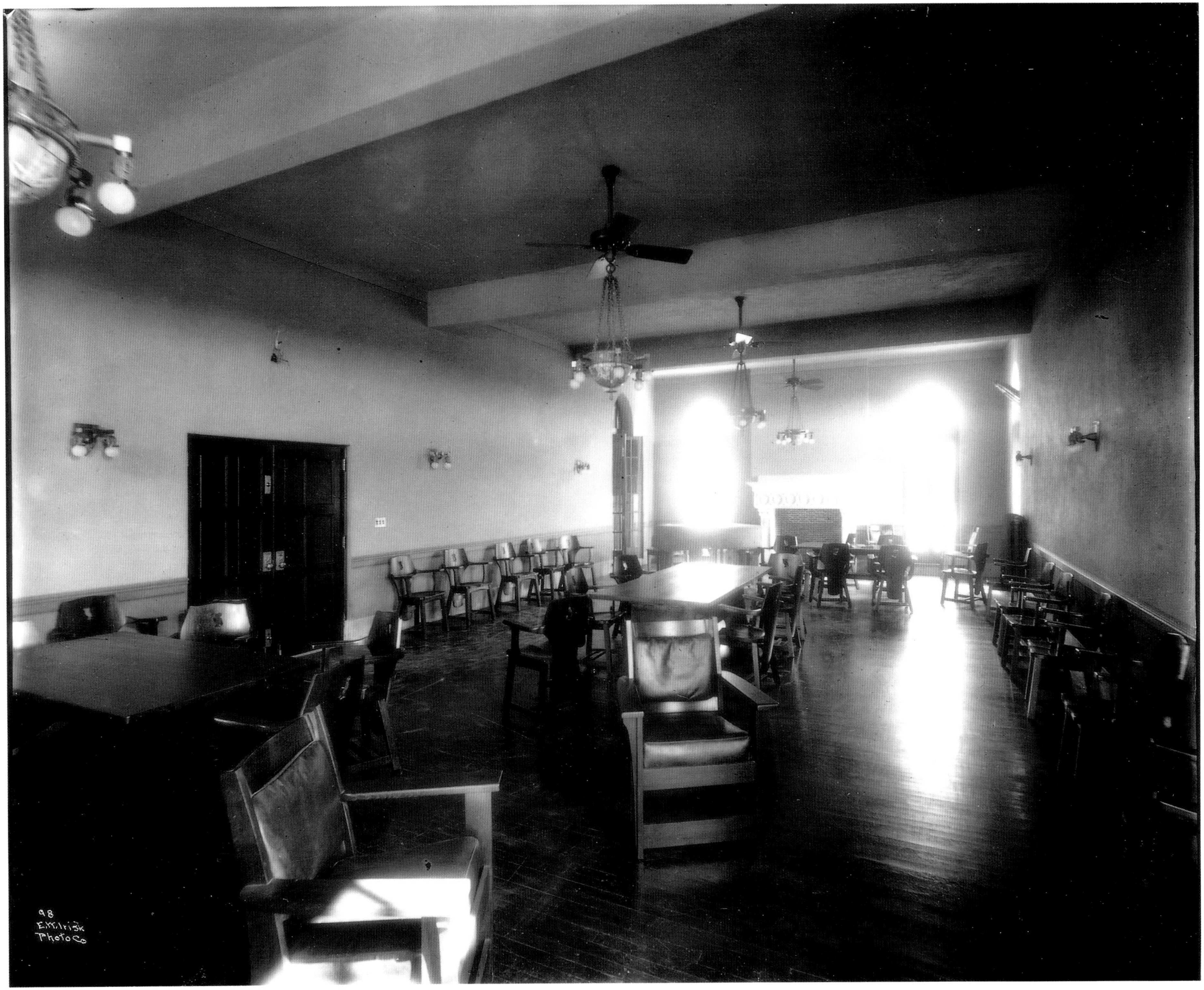
98
E.W. Irish
Photo Co

The seventy-fifth anniversary in 1987 of the opening of the Rice Institute provides an appropriate occasion to look at the university both retrospectively and prospectively. The past accomplishments of the institution and a commitment to excellence promise to guide all future development of Rice University. As President Rupp has said, the larger Rice community celebrates "the very substantial achievements of the University" and also shares "a sense that it can be even better. This sense of expectation is . . . indispensable as we build further on the great strengths that are here to realize even greater distinction in the years ahead." Rice has always been challenged by the remembrance of its founding. The new boldness of purpose in 1987 recalls the vision of 1912 and reminds one of the sense of wonder generated then by the university located in what was the most unlikely of places, the wide open spaces of Texas.

Rice remains a very small university in terms of enrollment, limited in size and so carefully planned that even the trees, which outnumber the students, are planted according to the dictates of design. While the endowment is rich in the proverbial Texas fashion, the university seems remarkably un-Texan: the students hail from every state and many nations, and more faculty have received their doctorates from foreign universities than from any single American university. The message conveyed vividly by the visual splendor of the campus—an obvious devotion to quality, a commitment to a founding concept, a genuine concern with human-scale activity, the sense of being in the midst of Houston, the world, and yet set apart by the hedges—renders with the truth of poetic vision what Rice is ultimately all about. Here, in the words of Edgar Odell Lovett, is an institution that "aspires to university standing of the highest grade."

—*John B. Boles*

Administration Building, cloisters, 1912

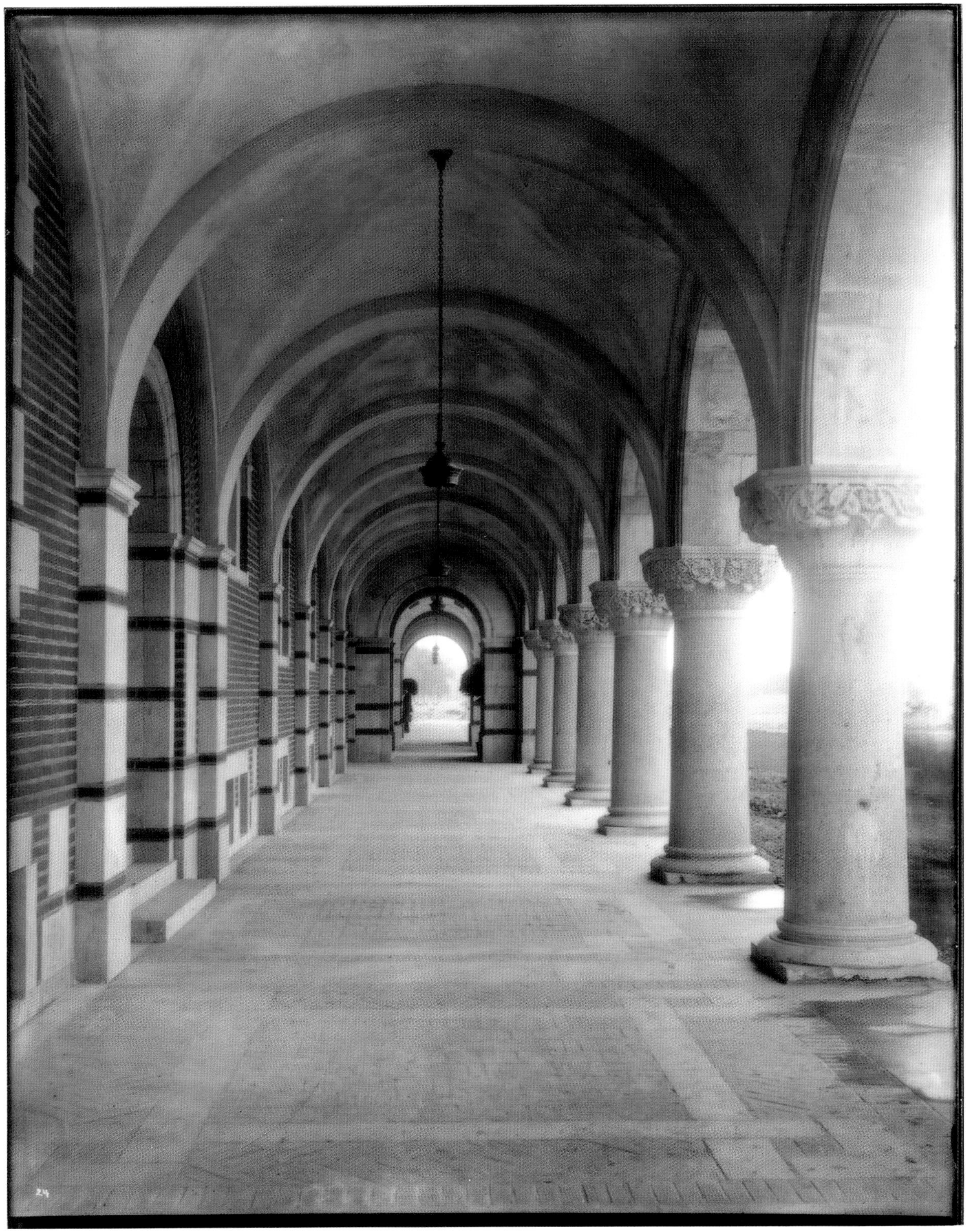

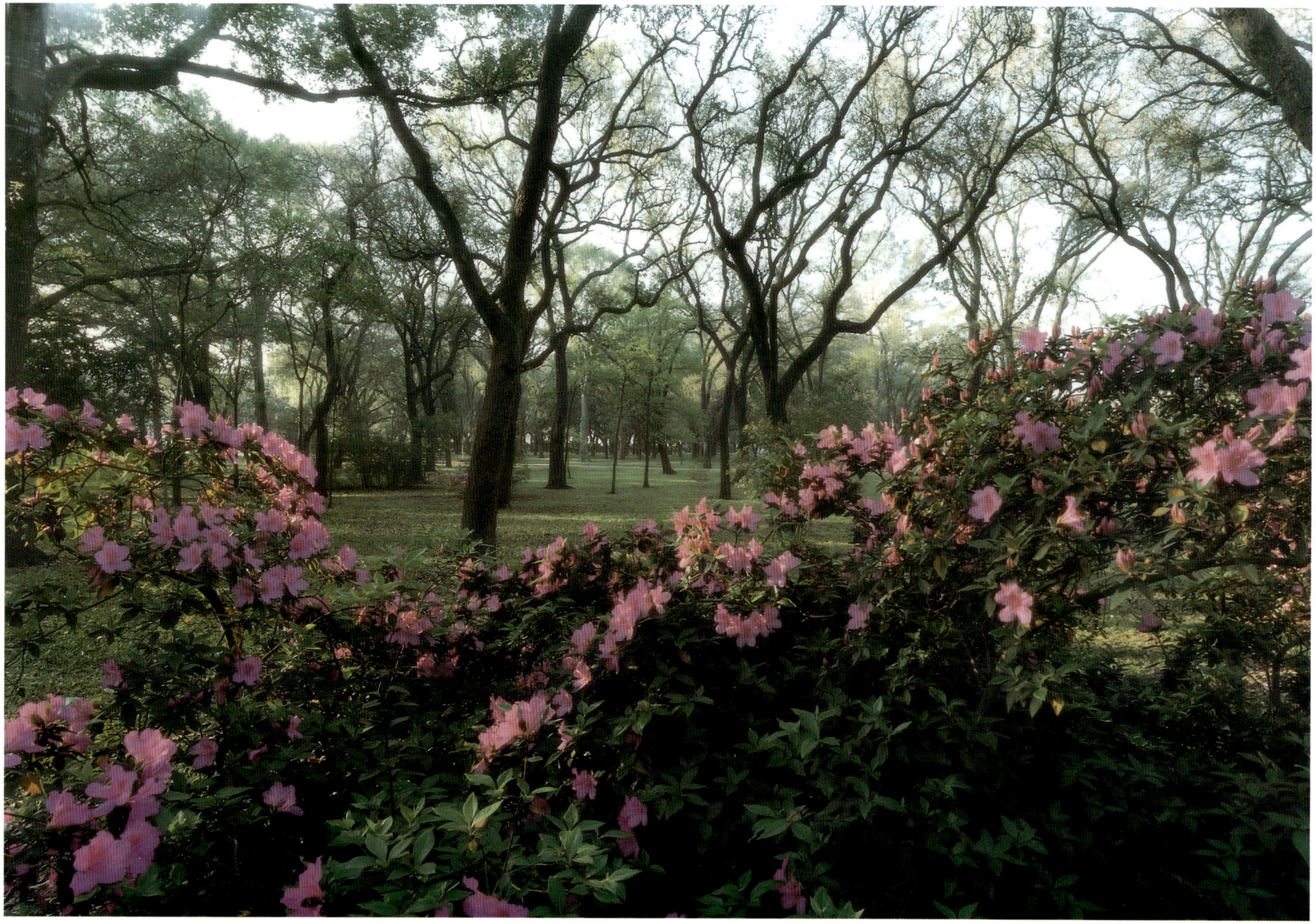

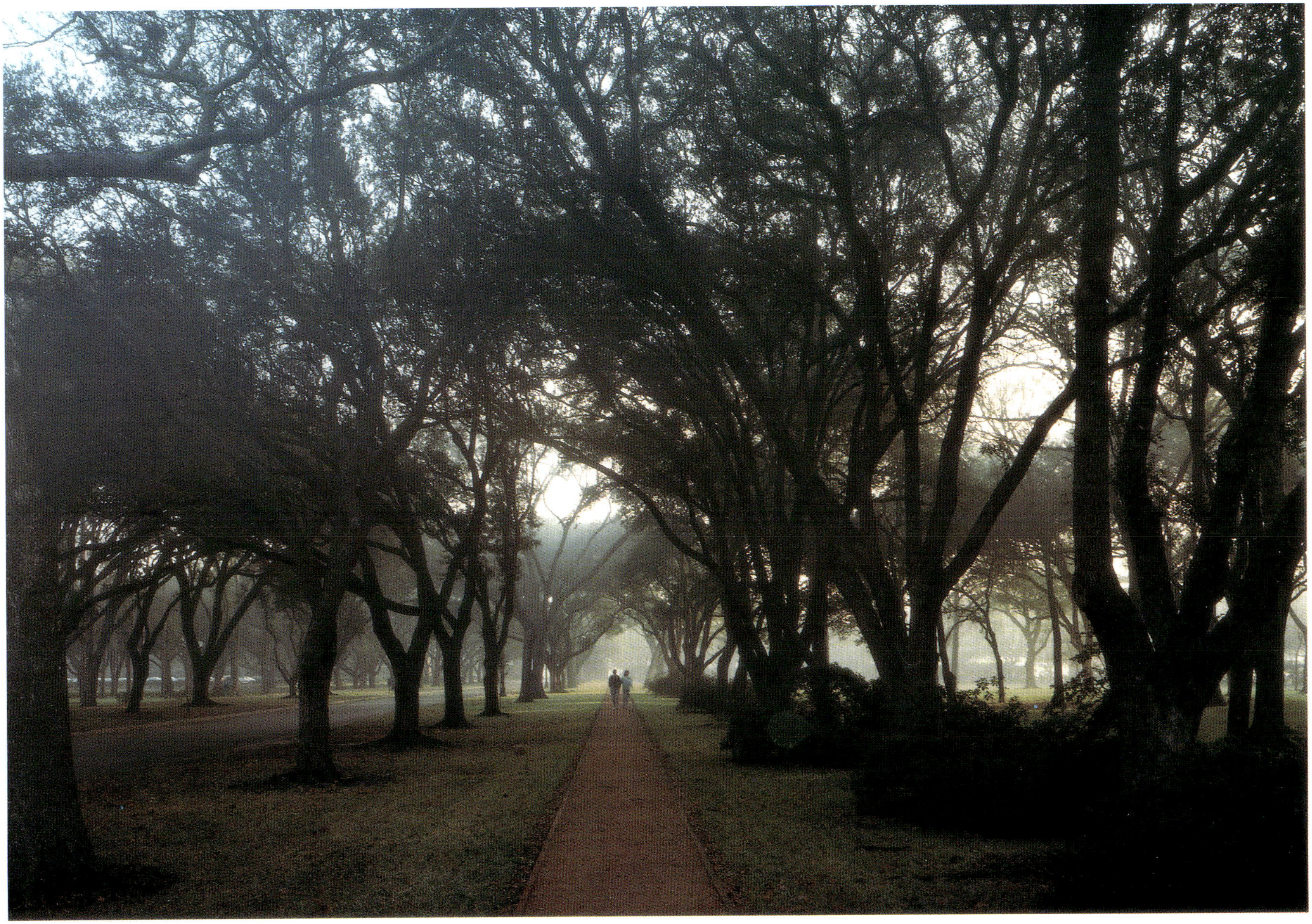

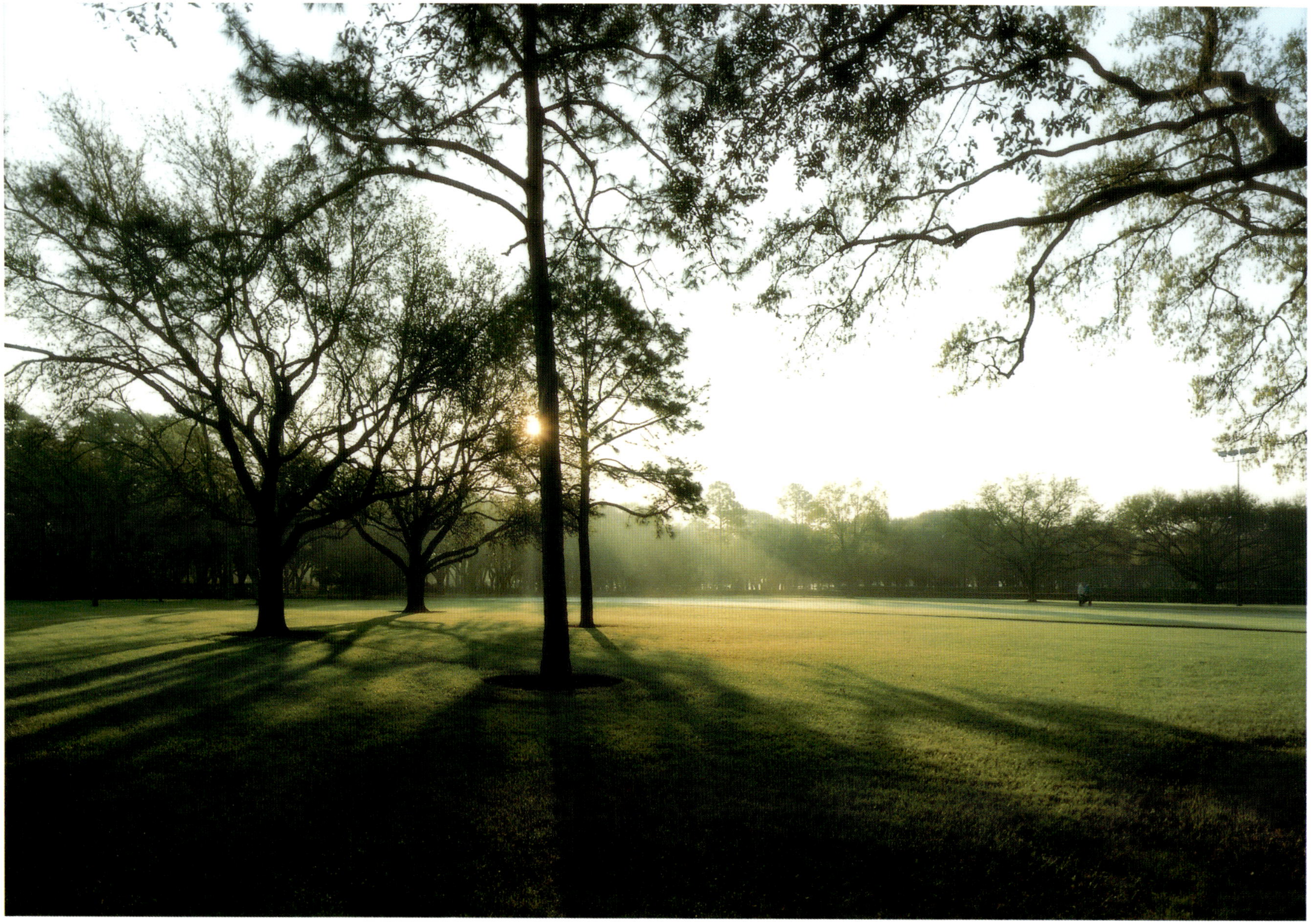

Oak trees and azaleas, southeast façade of Lovett Hall

Heizer sculpture and the Mechanical Engineering Building

Physics Building and the academic court

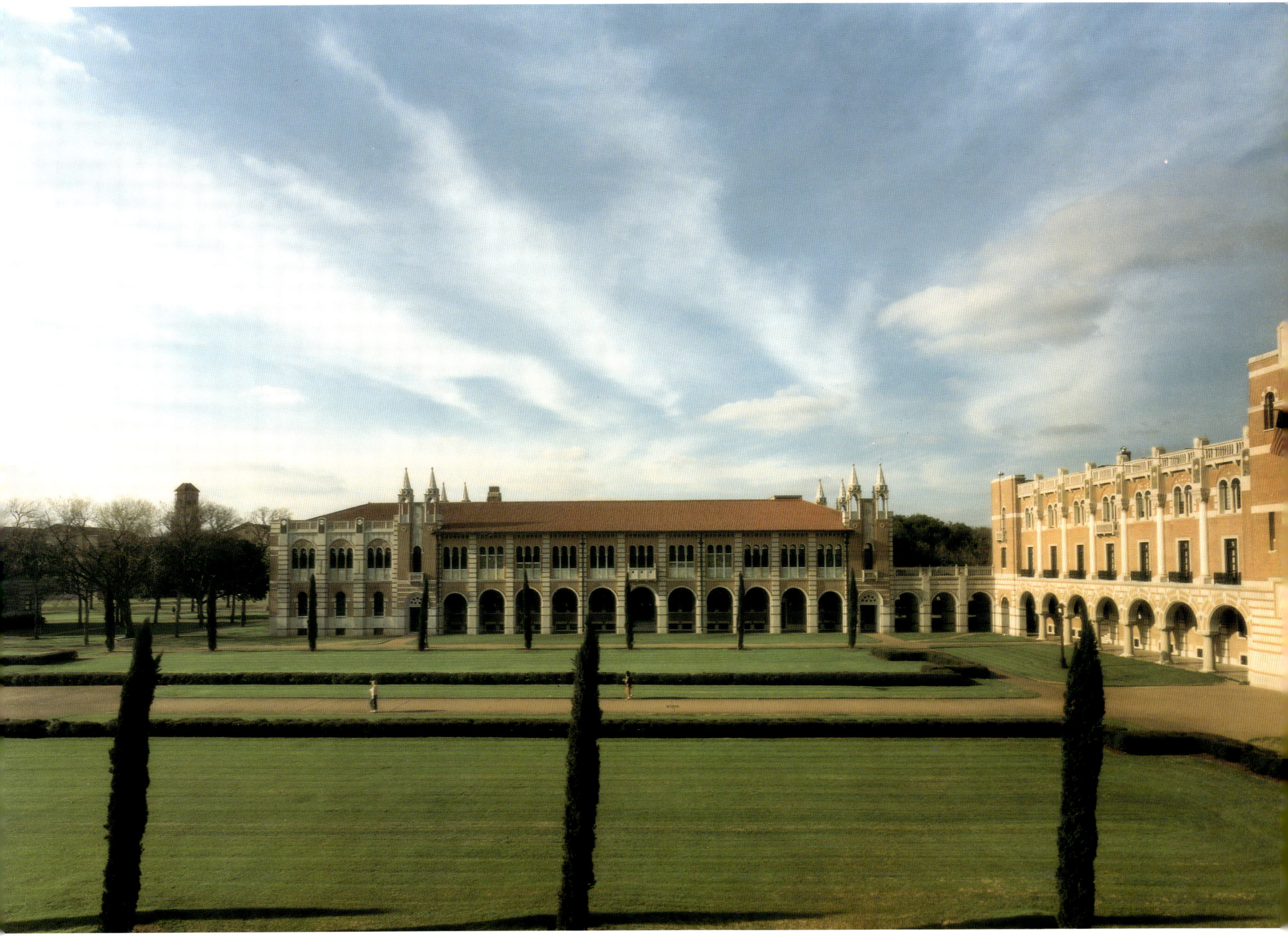

Baker College quadrangle

Herring Hall

Academic Court

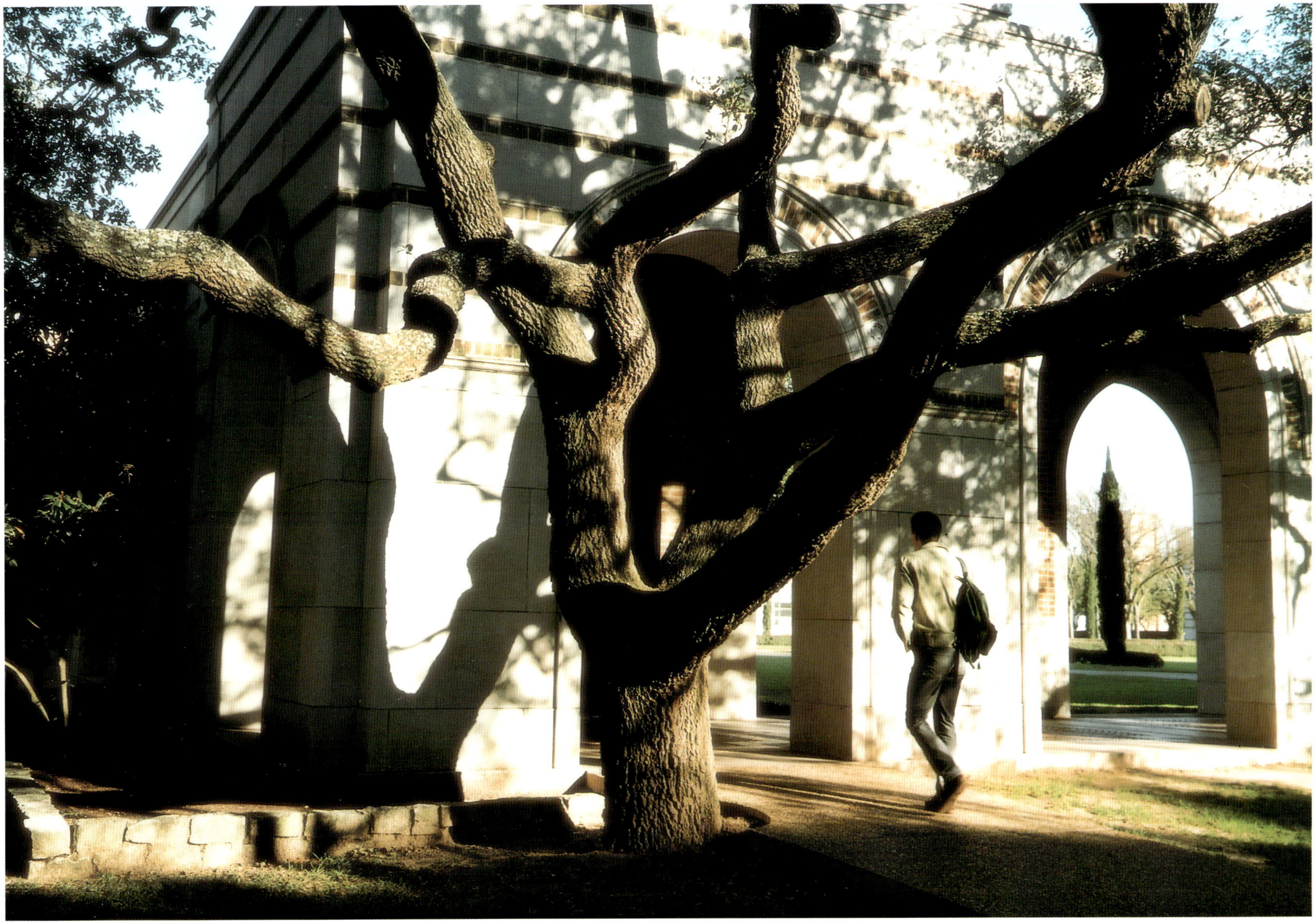

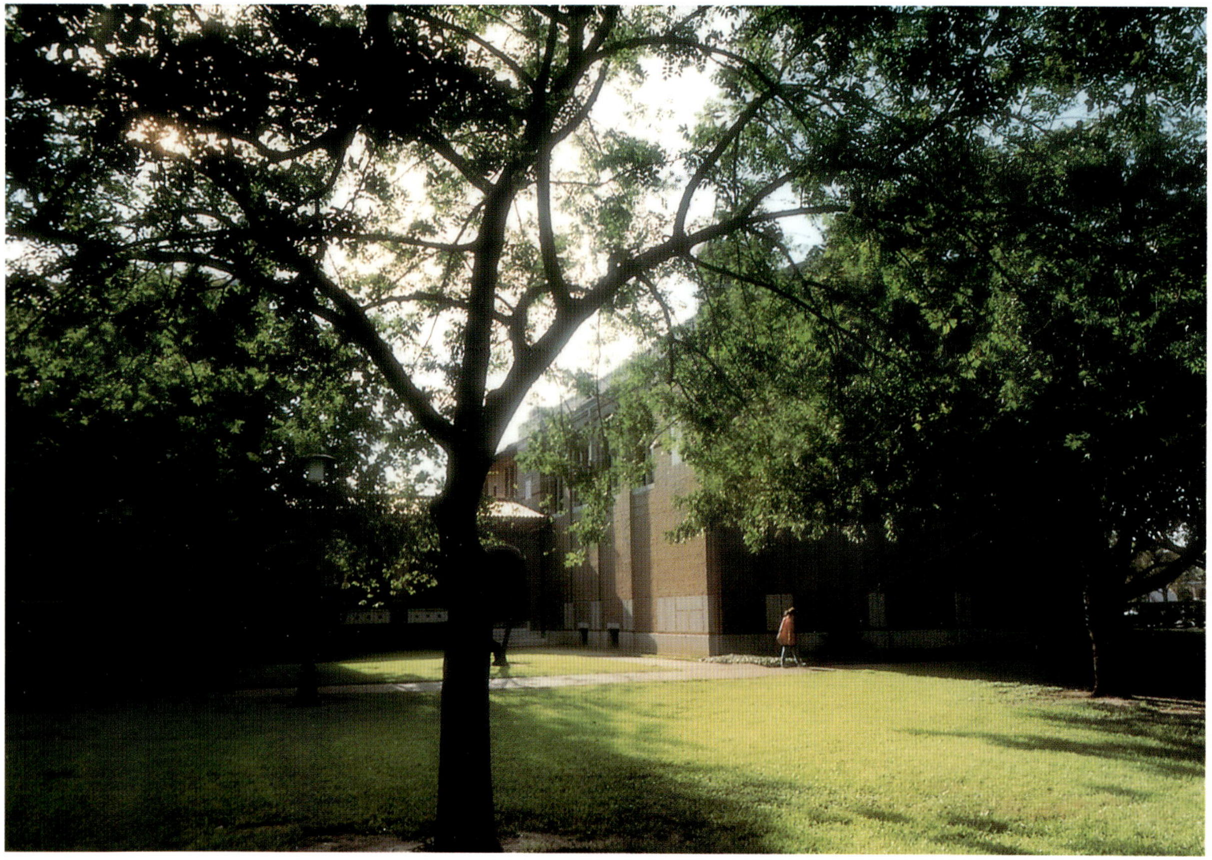

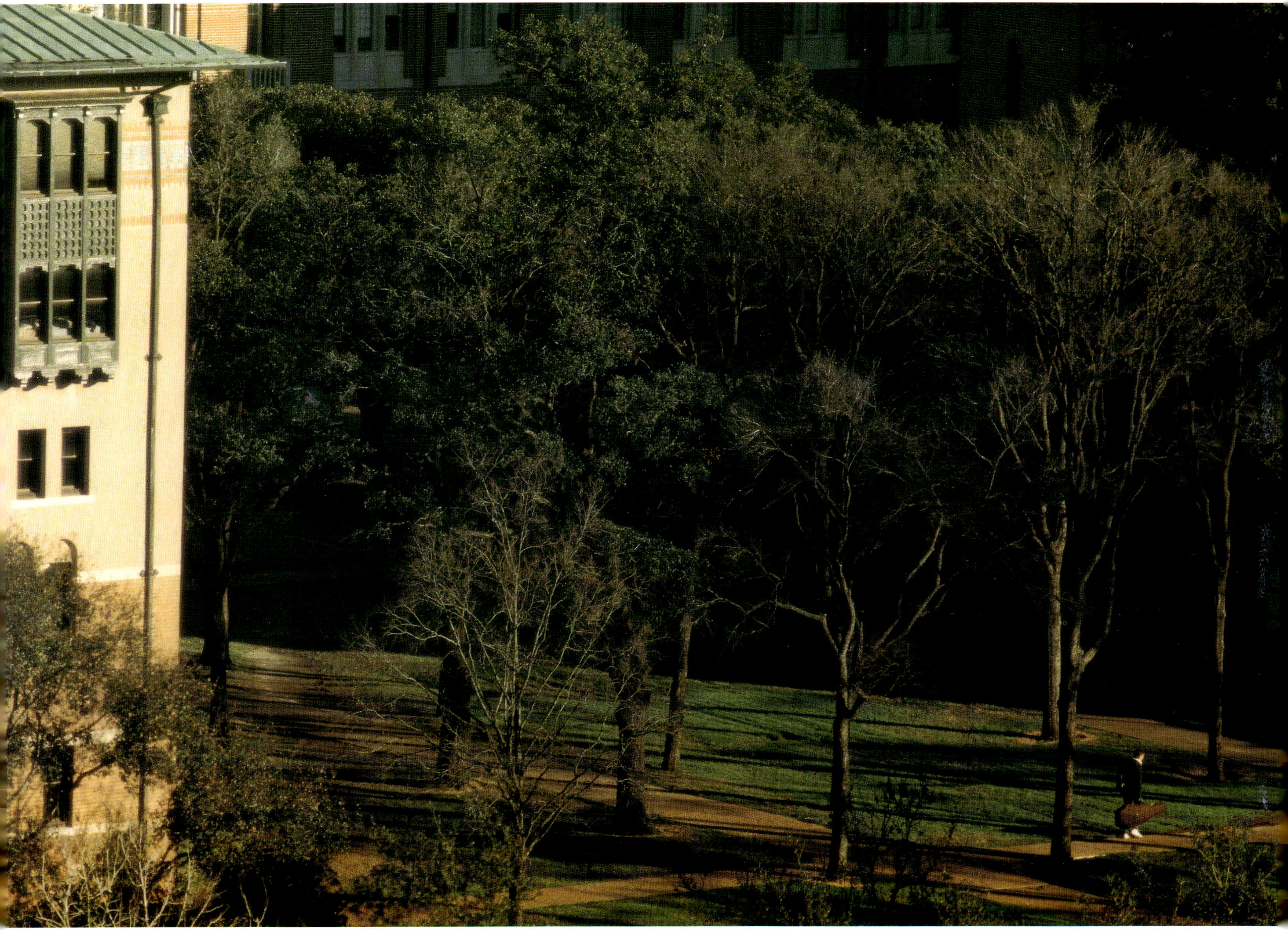

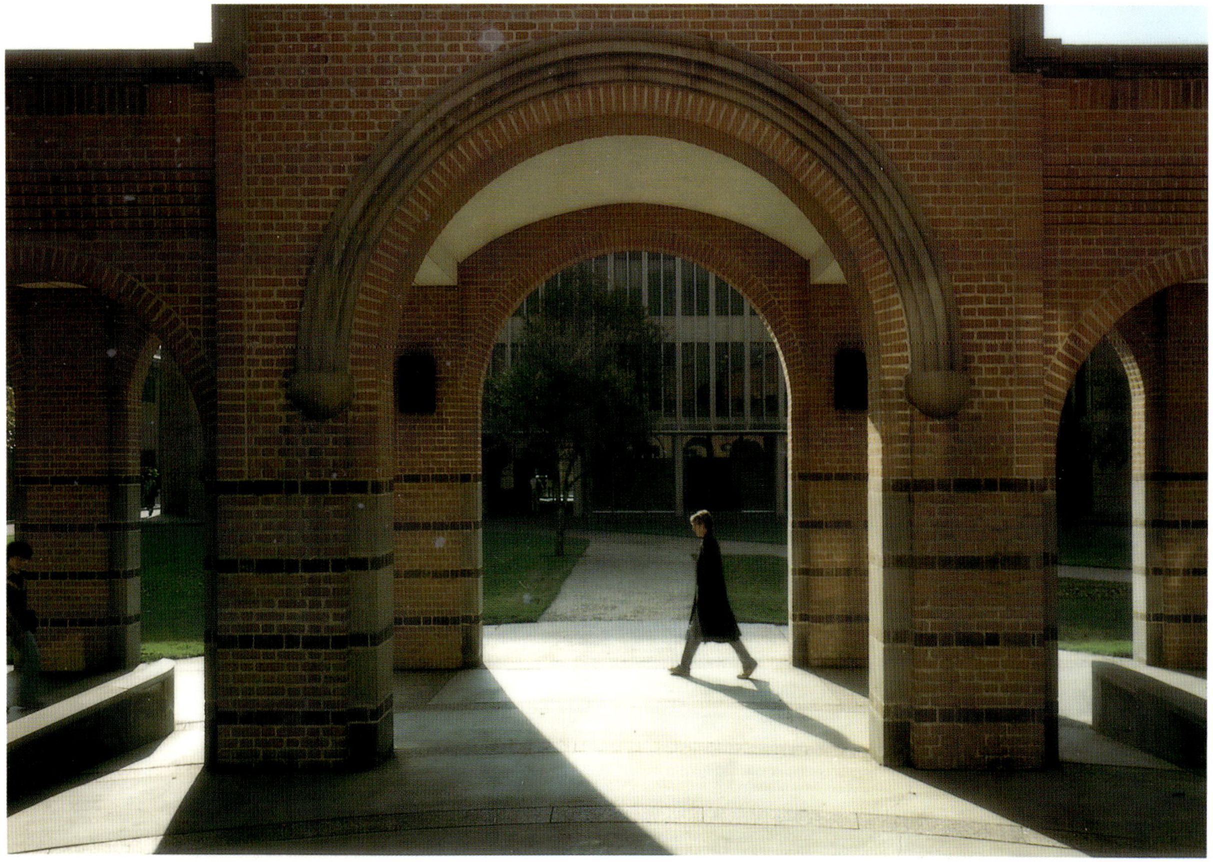

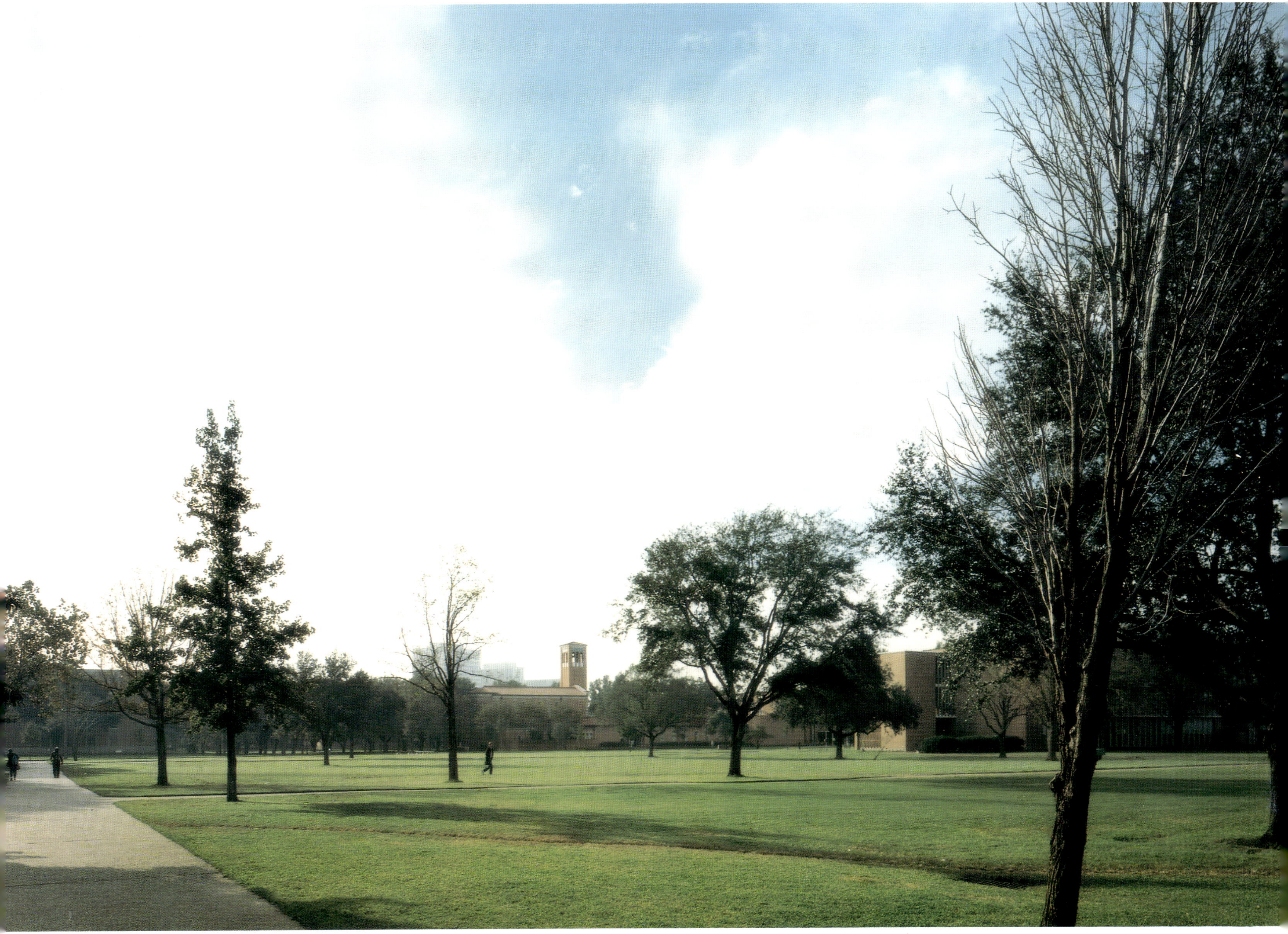

50

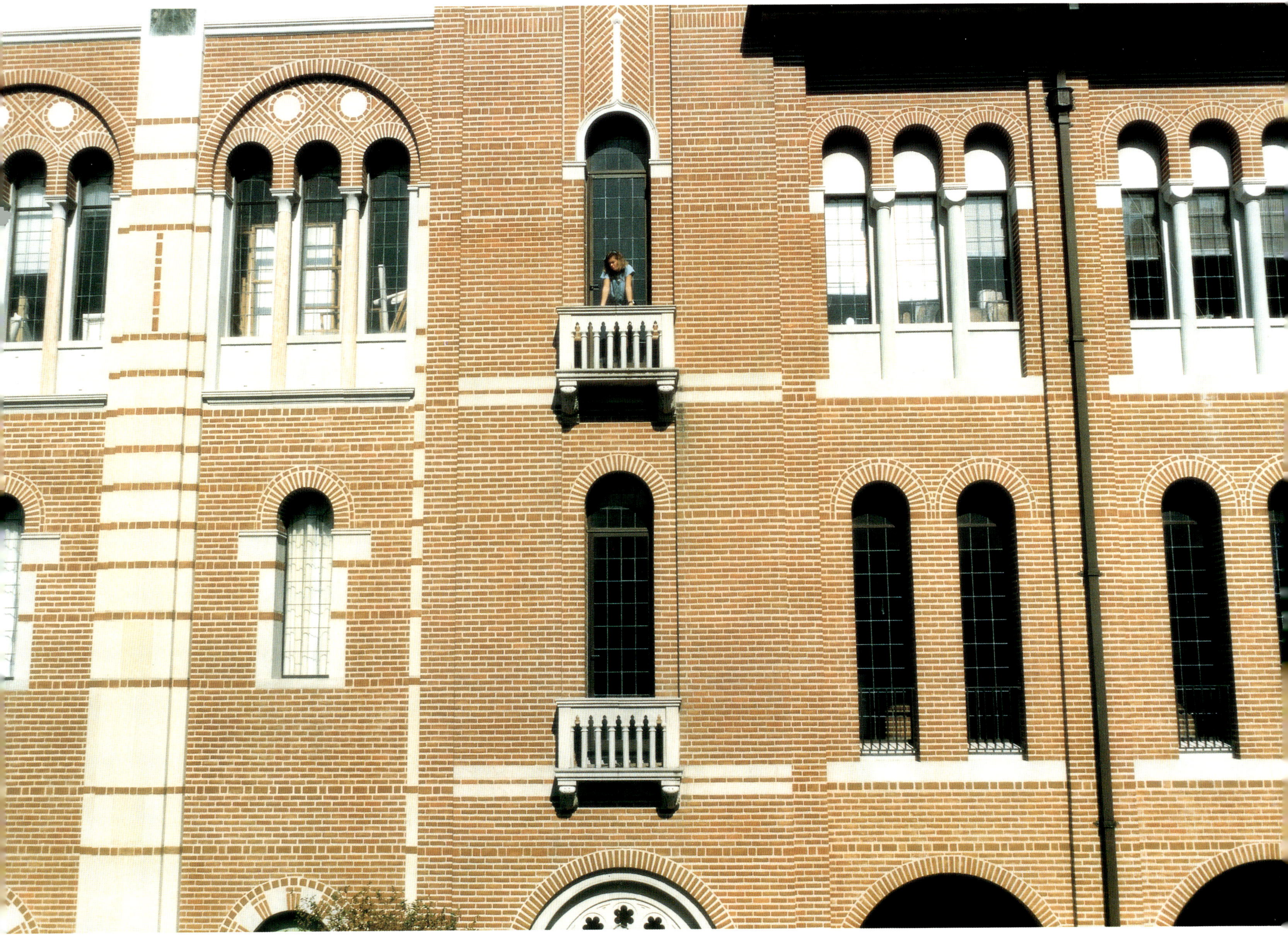

College opened a window on the great world beyond my flat West Texas horizons. I arrived at Rice in September 1960, fresh from high school in the Panhandle town of Plainview. That fall Kennedy and Nixon campaigned in Houston. After the election, President Eisenhower came to Rice and delivered his valedictory warning about the military-industrial complex. I had grown up with the *Lubbock Avalanche-Journal,* but some of my more sophisticated Rice classmates read the *New York Times,* and there were professors who referred to newspapers like the *Times* of London, *Le Monde,* and the *Frankfurter Allgemeine Zeitung.* The air was thick with names I had never heard, books I had never read, ideas I had never imagined. It was intimidating and exhilarating.

The popular teachers were often, though not always, Young Turks new to Rice. Typically, the young professors arrived with Ph.D.s from more prestigious universities and mixed emotions about living and teaching in Houston—because it was Southern, because it was hot, because they feared that the academic world that really mattered would not take them seriously. But they were good teachers, and they were accessible to their students. In class they explicated "The Waste Land," analyzed American economic growth, or unlocked the secrets of international diplomacy. Then they held forth on everything from music to baseball over coffee in the student center or at dinner in the residential colleges. We weren't required to accept their views, but it was obvious we had to learn their methods.

Sometime during my sophomore year my education started making sense to me. It wasn't just committing mountains of facts to memory, though that played a part. I remember waking up more than one night to find my roommate—an economics major taking pre-med courses—sitting up in bed, eyes open but sound asleep, reciting carbon-chain formulas for his organic chemistry class. And it went beyond acquiring skills like French and German for me, or comparative anatomy and microeconomic analysis for him.

It had more to do with developing critical habits of mind—an unfamiliar notion for many of us when we first arrived on campus. In high school in the fifties, most authorities (including teachers) acted as if our society's received ideas and conventional wisdom were so brittle they had to be protected.

Humanities lecture

At Rice, in stark contrast, little was sacred and almost everything was up for discussion. That took some getting used to. Here we were, many of us raw youths from the five corners of Texas, expected to question authors' assumptions, dissect great works of literature, comment on world-historical events, debate the existence of God, even argue with professors—some professors, anyway.

Most former students, if they try, can recall when the light began to dawn. For me it happened in a year-long course on Europe since the Renaissance. Emotionally, history is the least congenial discipline for the young, inclined as they are—as we were—to assume that time began the day before yesterday and that only the future matters. But intellectually, any attempt to understand the present pushes us back toward the past.

The two professors who shared the teaching duties could hardly have been less alike. One, a tall, angular, laconic Canadian, delivered precise, detached lectures that laid bare the anatomy of the past like medical-school dissections. He would crook his body over his index cards like a living question mark, then raise his head and peer at his audience through thick eyeglasses that I sometimes imagined were historical microscopes. The other was a short, restless, emotional Ivy Leaguer with a machine-gun lecturing style, a provocative taste for historical analogy, and a keen sense of disaster past, present, and impending—appropriate enough, given the subject matter.

Listening first to one and then the other, I slowly began to perceive the dim movement of cause and effect behind the screen of facts, dates, and textbook clichés I had taken for history. By spring, when we reached the First World War and studied the upheavals that shaped the forbidding landscape of this century, I was catching on. I remember sitting in the cool auditorium for lectures, then emerging into Houston's stifling heat, lost in discussion with classmates as excited as I was by our fledgling attempts at analysis. I never looked at the world the same way again.

Physics lecture, Physics amphitheater

Painting and watercolor class

Architecture studio, Anderson Hall

English literature lecture, Rayzor Hall

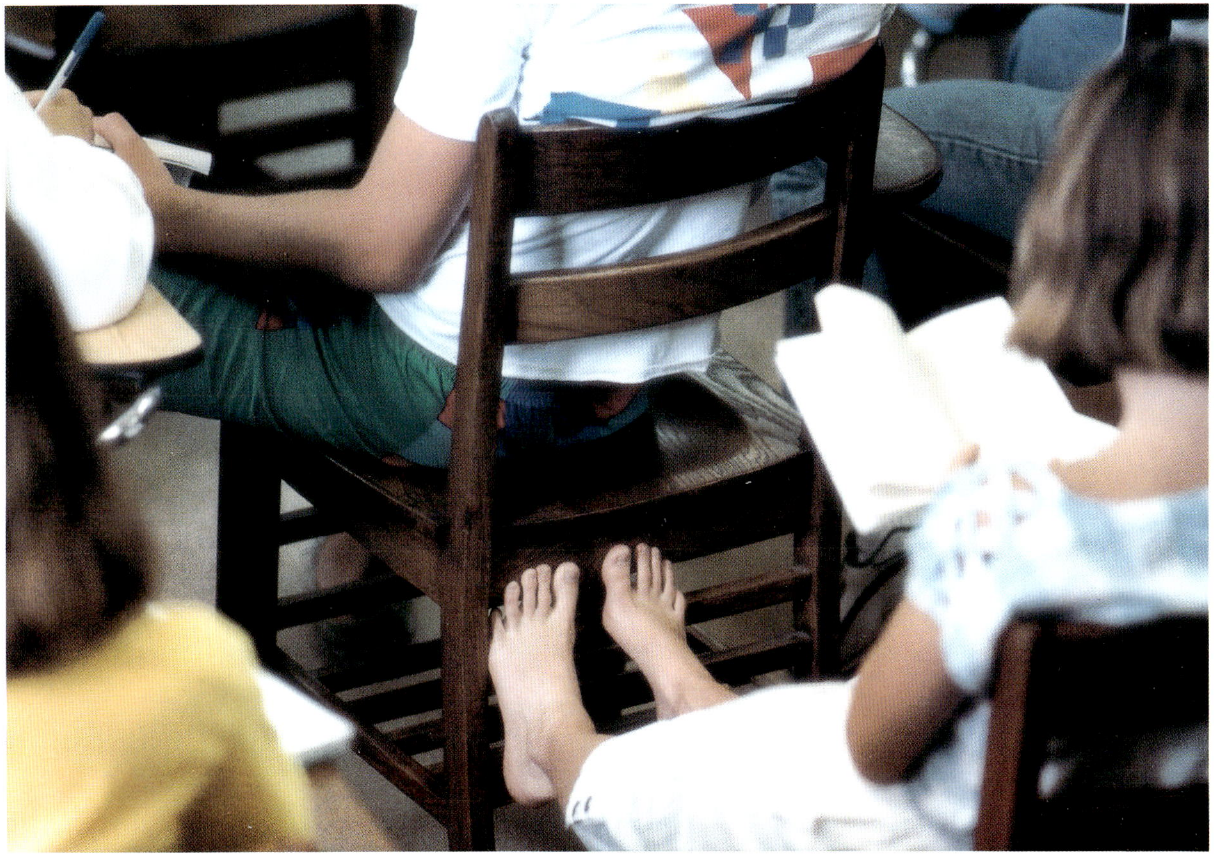

After a twenty-year absence I returned to Rice for a week in 1984. A lot has changed. There are now enough students to form a critical mass, and the residential college system, brand new when I was there, is flourishing. So today's campus is much livelier. On a November football weekend, in addition to the post-game parties, four different colleges as well as the Rice Players were presenting dramatic or musical pieces. I ended up watching a slick Hanszen College staging of a Stephen Sondheim revue. Since the university has no drama, journalism, or communications departments and provides little support other than the use of its facilities, student productions at Rice—including the weekly newspaper and the campus radio station—are true extracurricular, grassroots phenomena. Somehow, to me, that makes them count for more.

The eight colleges house around 250 students each. The college system offers a sensible residential and social alternative to the atomization of faceless dormitories and the cramped hierarchies of fraternities and sororities. These days the residential colleges are so popular that some students actually choose to live three to a two-person room, even though moving off campus can be cheaper.

The colleges play no formal academic role, but they have served as a meeting ground for students and faculty for nearly thirty years. Instead of eating at "high table" as in Cambridge and Oxford, Rice faculty associates mix with students at lunch and dinner. As a history major, where but in the Hanszen commons would I have gotten to know chemistry and engineering professors?

During my week back on campus, I sat in on a freshman English section that reminded me of similar scenes a couple of decades ago: a dozen bright kids, respectful to a fault, listening attentively to an energetic young professor's applied lesson in critical analysis—in this case, how to find and interpret symbolic and allegorical elements in *Deliverance,* a successful novel of the seventies which they probably suspected was more than just a good read.

I asked some of the faculty about Rice's campaign for greatness. One department head pointedly asked what the alternative was—planned mediocrity? "Some feel if you can't be Princeton or Yale, you shouldn't even try," he said, "but others of us don't agree." Several insisted on the school's unique identity: "We're not Princeton or Stanford or MIT, we're Rice." One of my former professors summed it up, "The things that work best at Rice are the things that matter most—students and teachers."

Then a senior, Class of '85, who spent his junior year in England on an exchange program with Cambridge University, told me that the best things about Rice are the other students, the availability of professors to undergraduates, and the residential college system. If someone had asked me in 1964, I'd have said the same.

—*Fryar Calhoun*

English literature seminar, Rayzor Hall

$$\left(\frac{\ell}{g}\right)^{1/2} = 2\pi\left(\left[\alpha(T-T_0)+1\right]g T_0^2/(4\pi^2 g)\right)^{1/2}$$

$$= T_0\left(\alpha(T-T_0)+1\right)^{1/2}$$

$$= (\Delta V) \quad 1\,\text{DAY}/(T_0 - \qquad \#\text{ticks}_{old} = \frac{86400\,\text{s/day}}{T_0/2} =$$

$$-V_{t_0}\left(1+\beta_{steel}\Delta T\right) = \Delta V$$

$$\left(\beta_{gas}-\beta_{st}\right)\Delta T = \Delta V \qquad \#\text{tick}_{(new)} = \frac{86400\,\text{s/da}}{T/2} =$$

Blackboard, Physics Building

Painting studio, Sewall Hall

Architecture studio, Anderson Hall

Main stage, Jones Hall

Design class, Sewall Hall

Symphony rehearsal, Hamman Hall

Chemistry laboratory

Symphony rehearsal

Painting and sculpture studios, Sewall Hall

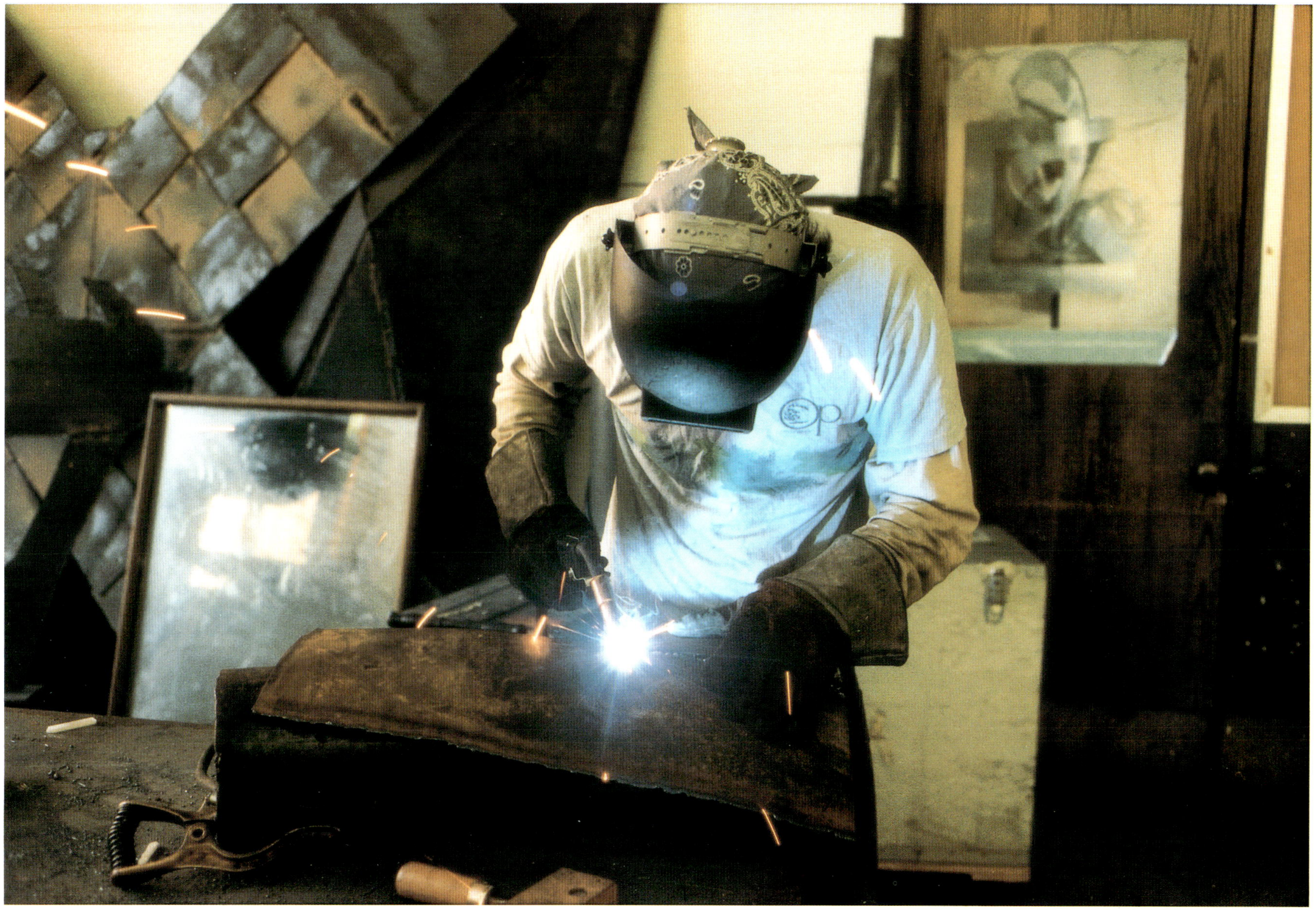

Professor of Political Science in his office

Inspecting a vacuum chamber,
Space Science Building

74

Stone carvings, Chemistry Building

75

Percussion studio, Hamman Hall

Sculpture studio, Sewall Hall

Chemistry laboratory

ROTC drills

Metastable de-excitation spectroscopy, Rice Quantum Institute

Electron capture spectroscopy, Rice Quantum Institute

Physics laboratory

Master violin class, Milford House

84

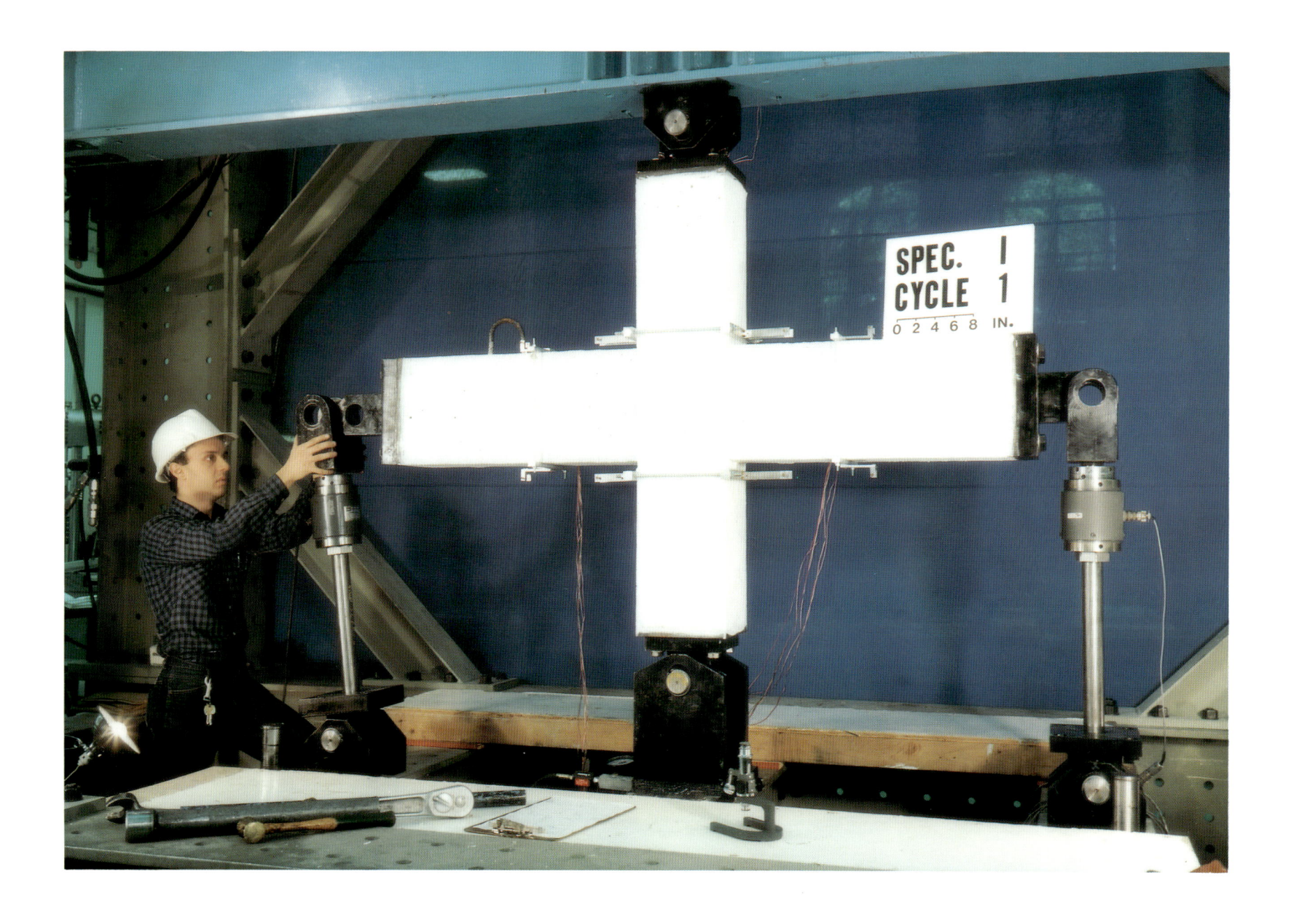

Stress testing concrete beams, Civil Engineering Department

Graduate research project, Chemistry Department

Filmmaking class, Media Center

King Lear, *Baker College*

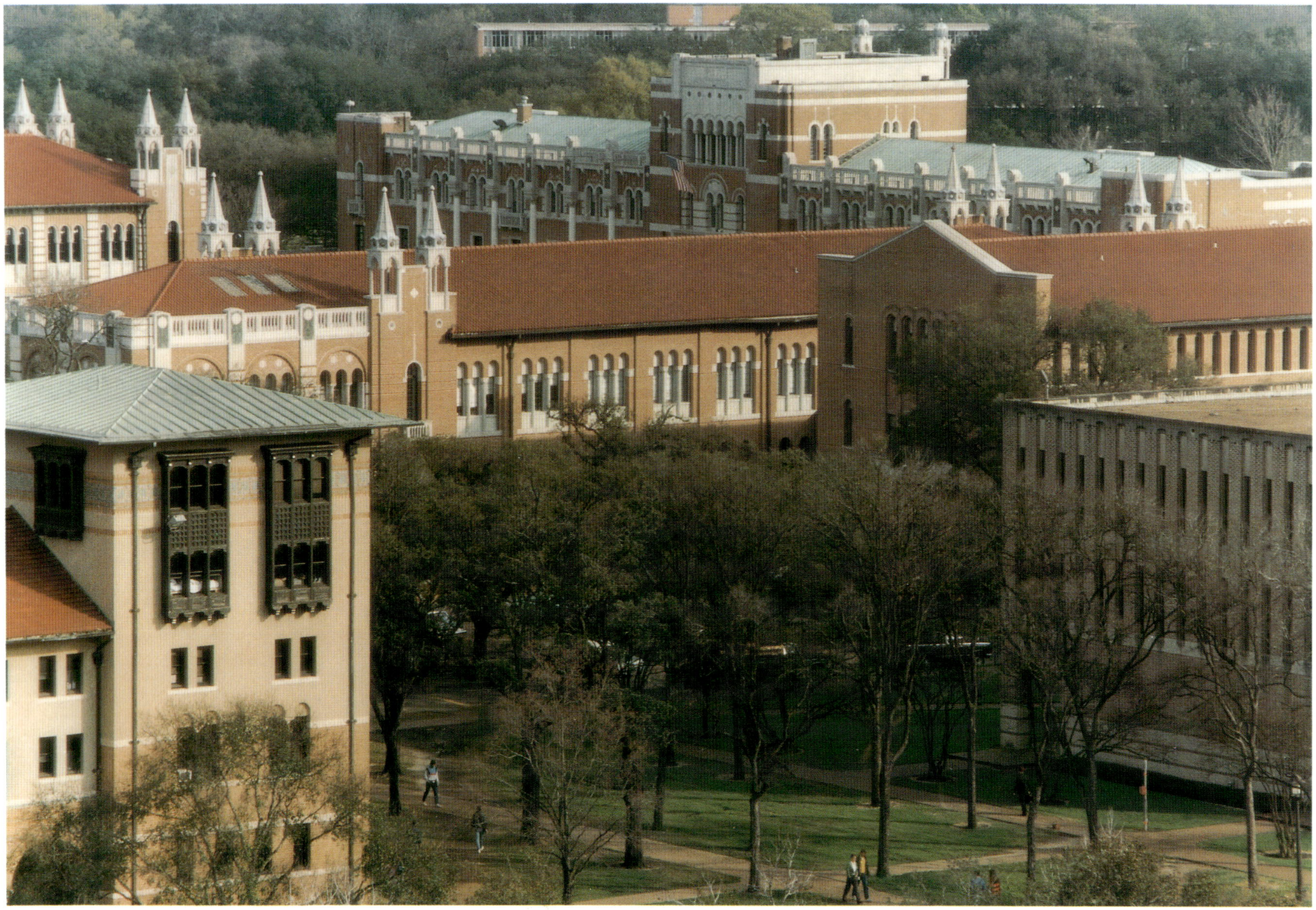

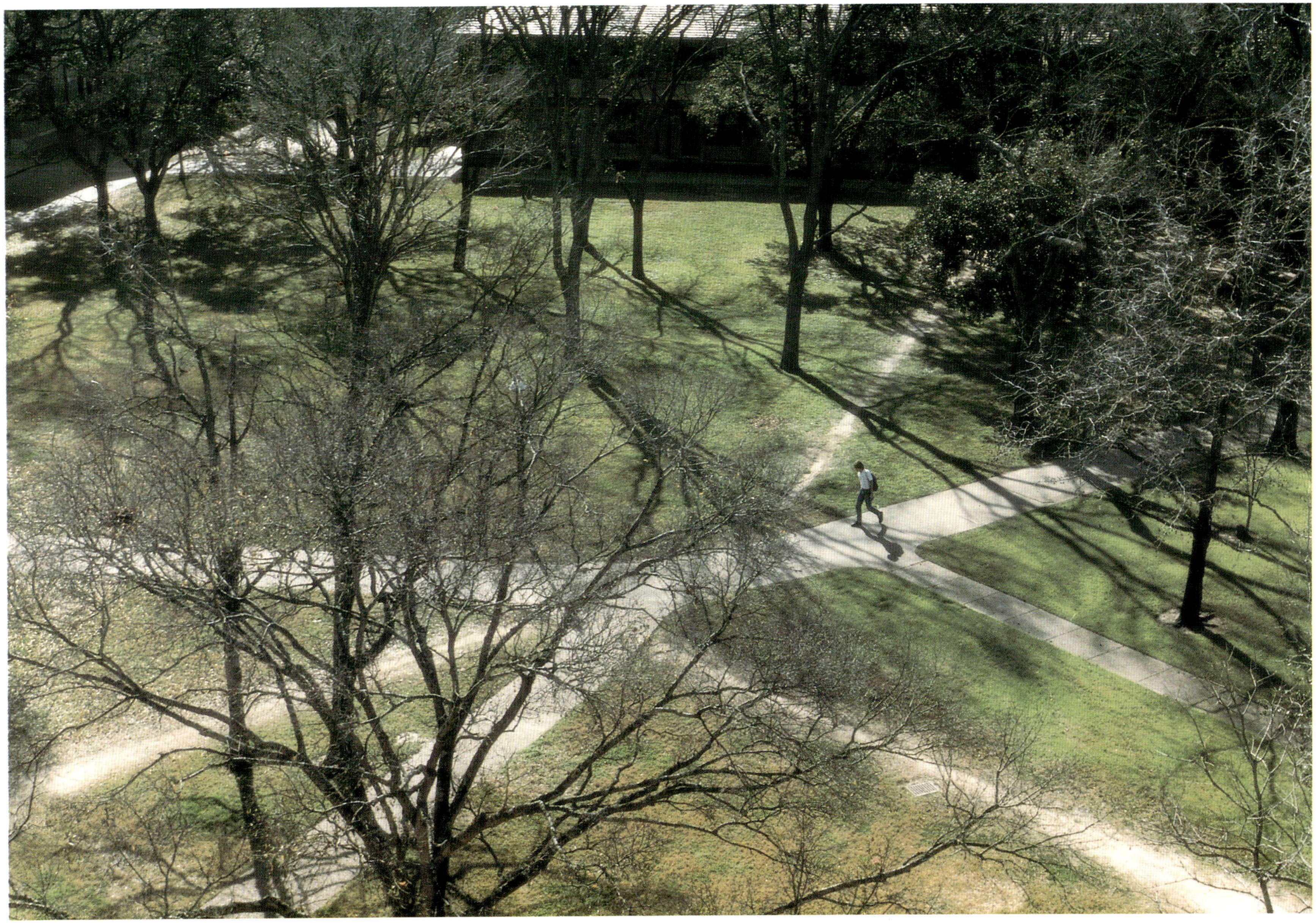

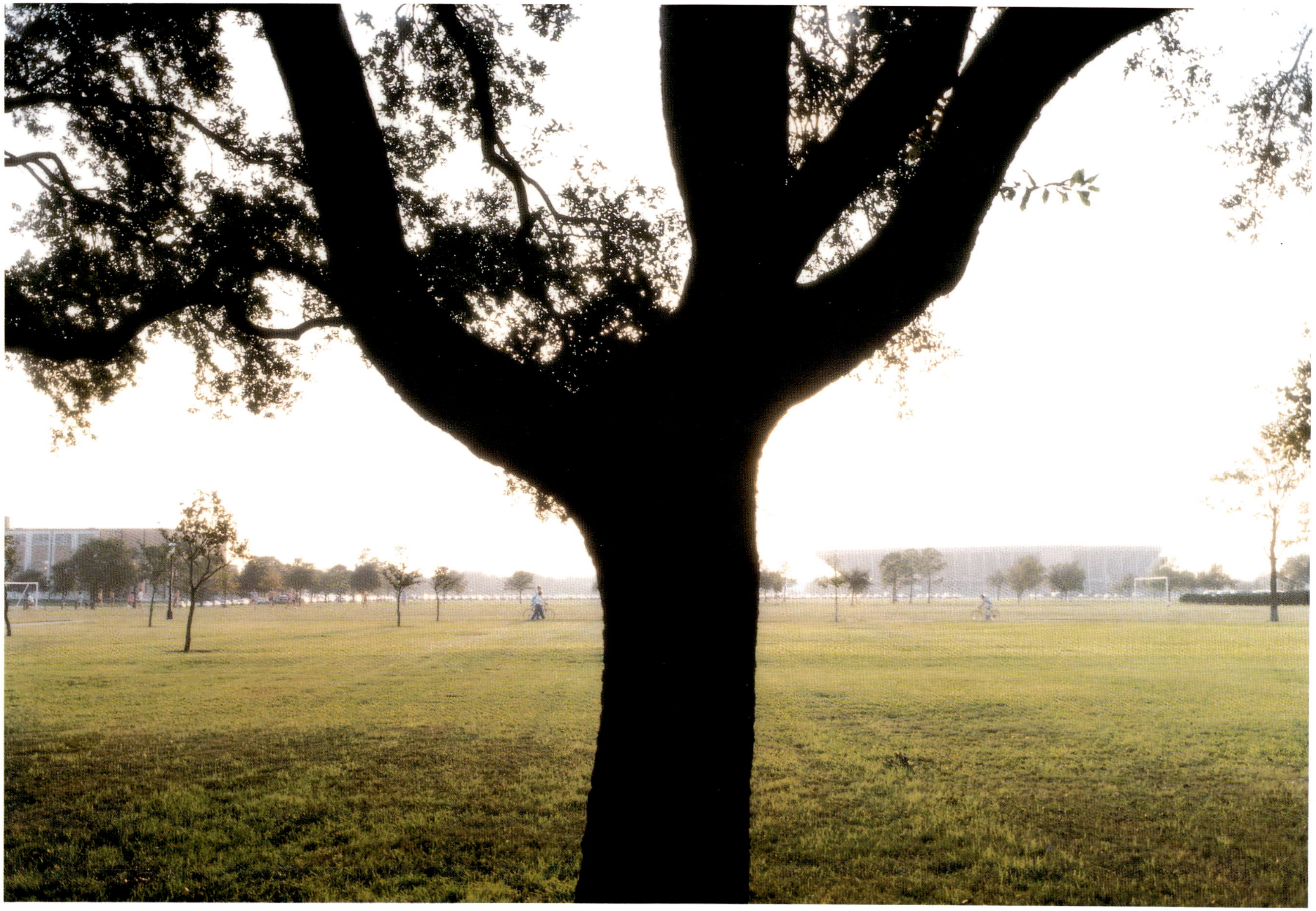

Intramural football

Stone carving, Baker College

93

Stone carving, Lovett Hall

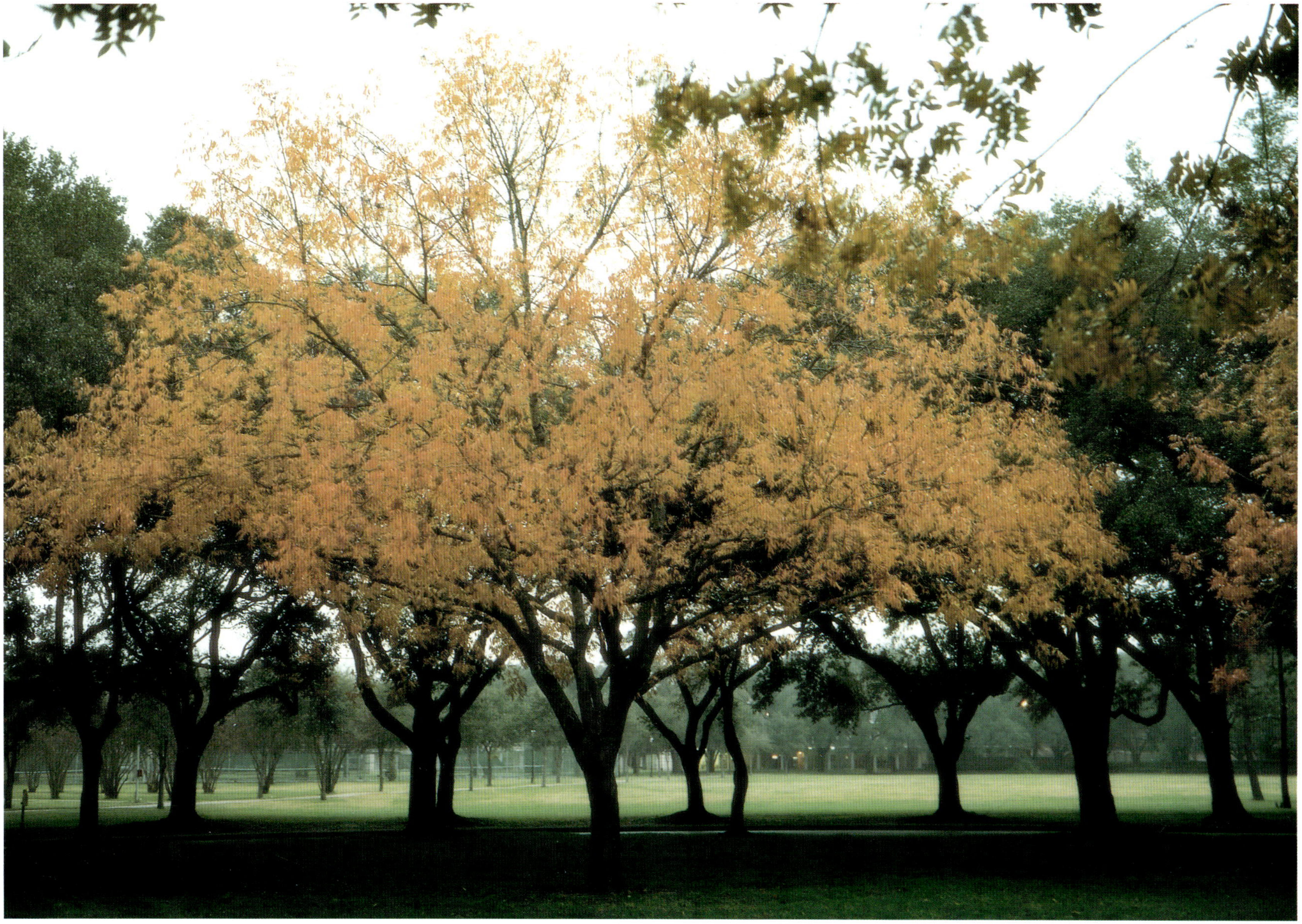

Lovett Hall and Physics Building, cloisters

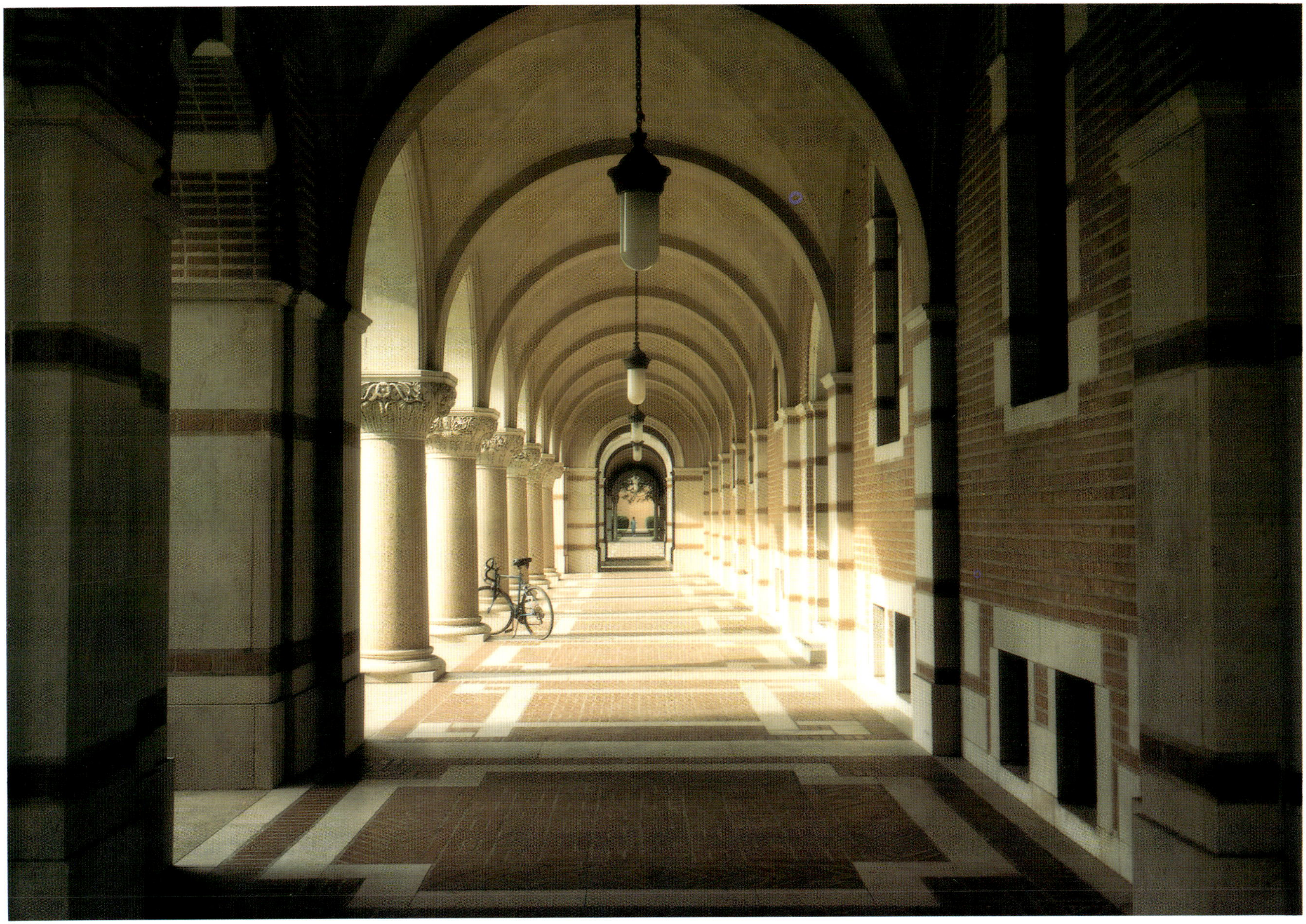

Academic court in the fog

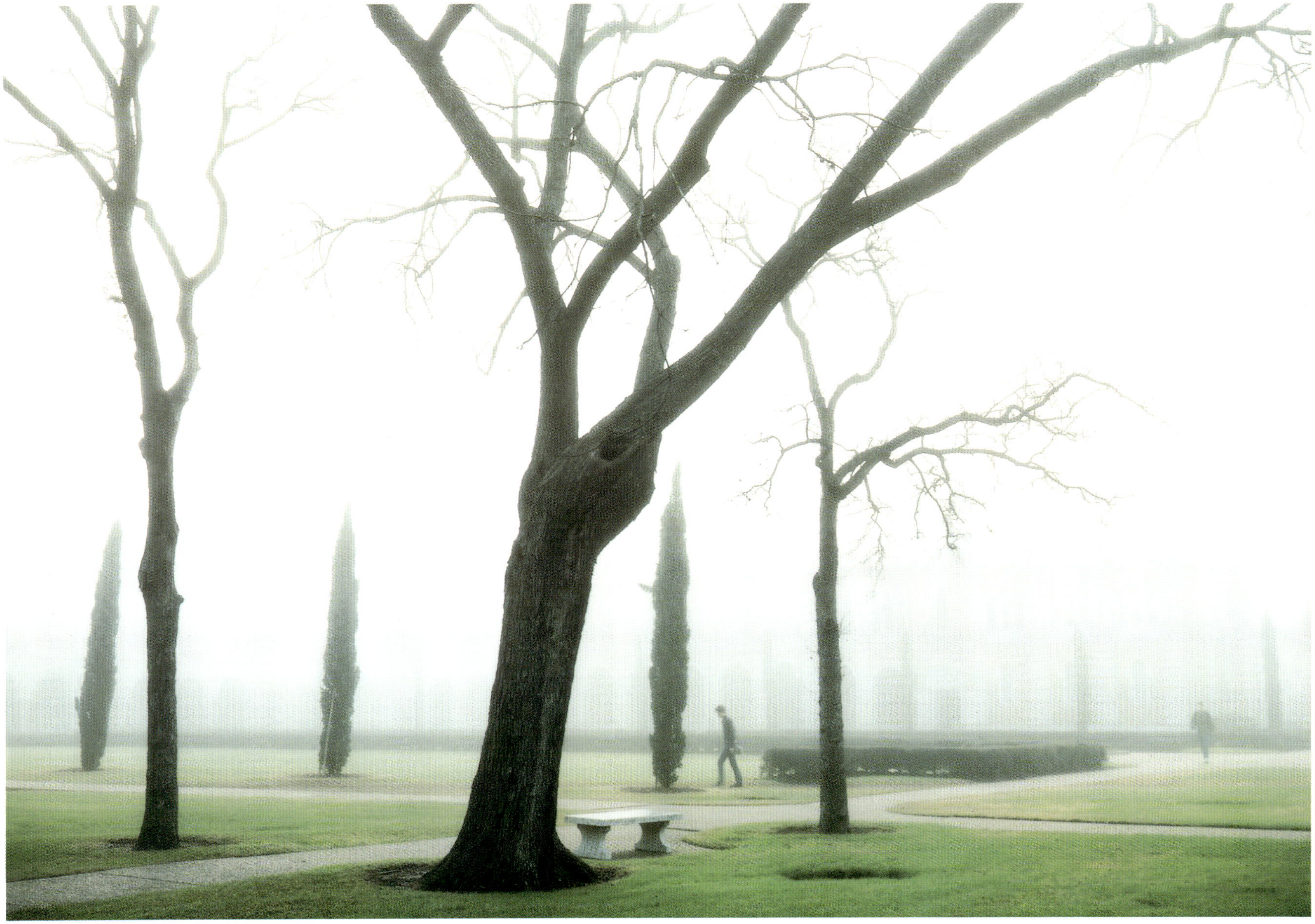

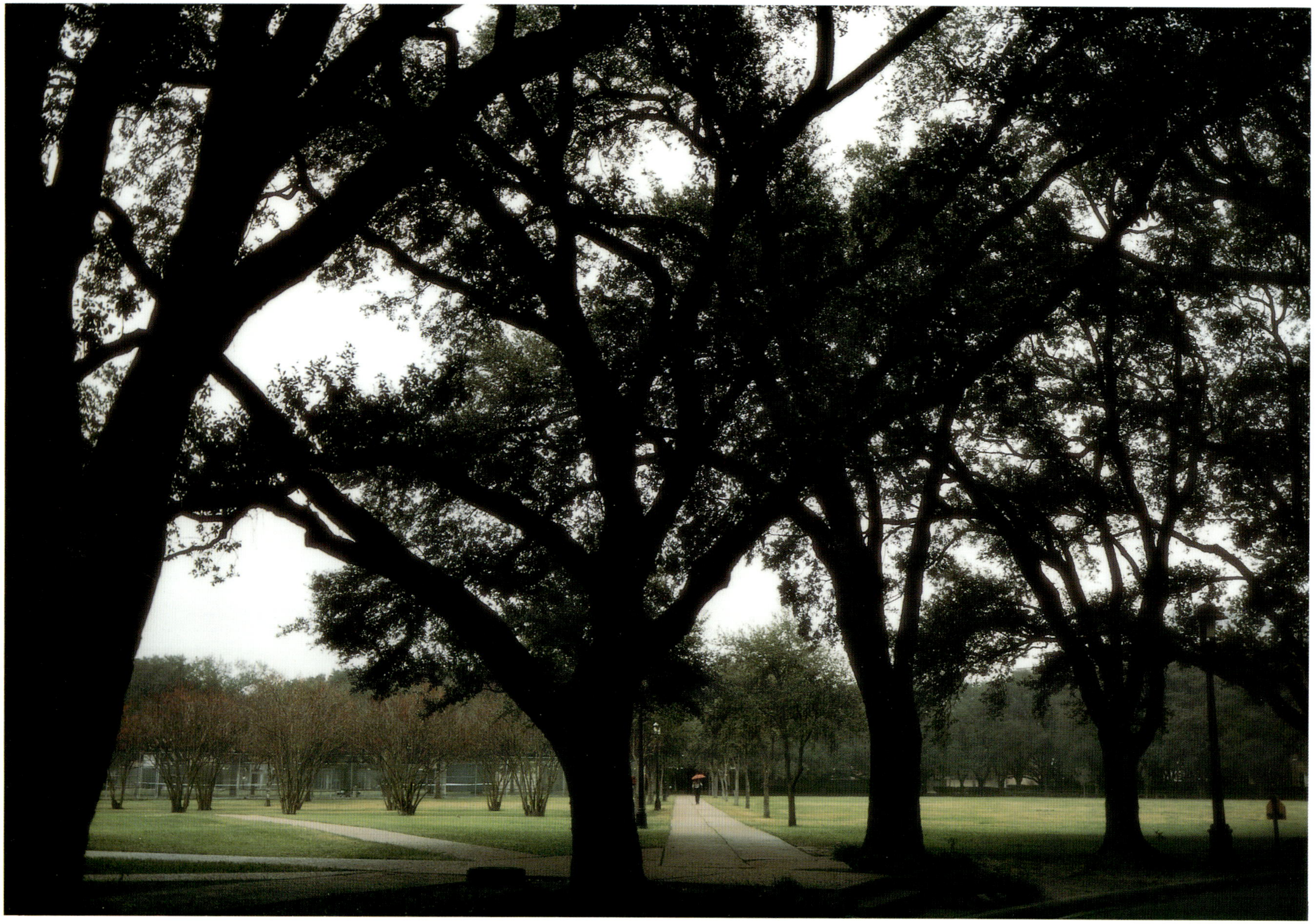

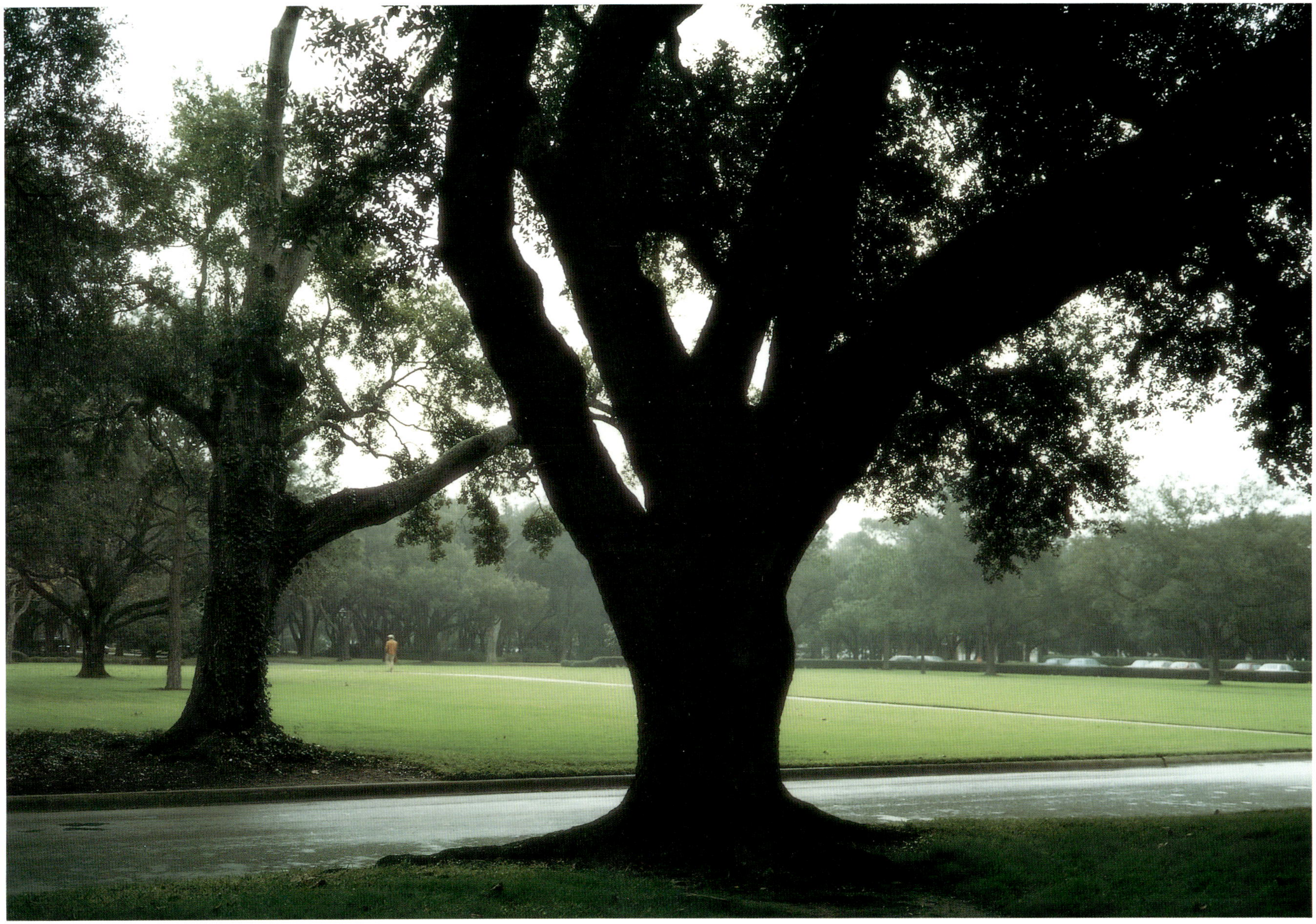

Rice students have always taken pride in working hard and playing hard, puncturing the swollen balloon of academic sobriety as a way of dealing with the stress. In my day that meant keeping your sense of humor intact, saving up barbs for the April Fool's Day issue of the *Thresher*, swatting mosquitoes on a humid May night at a Colt 45's game in the pre-Astros era, and hearing Ray Charles in a segregated Houston concert where whites were restricted to one corner of the stands and kept off the dance floor.

Rice has always had its share of college high-jinks. A prank from the 1920's, in which the freshman class president hid for two days in the ceiling of the Turnverein Club in order to crash the sophomore prom, is immortalized in a humorous terracotta panel on the wall of Will Rice, one of the residential colleges. The pajama-clad freshman "Slime Parade" through downtown Houston was another tradition of the early years. While I was there an ingenious student threw Baker College into a turmoil by tampering with the power supply and making all the clocks run faster. These days Rice's annual spring beer-bike relay race is about as rowdy as the goldfish-swallowing rituals of yesteryear.

There's nothing unusual about this part of Rice student tradition—just the opposite. Late adolescent silliness is a way for Rice students to show that they are like students everywhere. It's a public proclamation that they refuse to devote every last bit of their energy to the serious business of matriculation, education, maturation, examination, and certification.

Club 13

A contemporary rite I observed last year supports this point. The free spirits of Baker College celebrate the 13th of each month (or the 26th, which is twice 13, or the 31st, which is 13 reversed) by racing through the nocturnal campus clad only in sneakers, beanies, and copious gobs of shaving cream. So what? The campus policeman who followed along and kept a discreet eye on things looked bored, and when the revelers briefly invaded the library, busy scholars hardly looked up from their books. Aside from the couple of dozen young men and women wearing Rapid Shave, I may have been the only person interested. A token audience is necessary for this sort of stunt, but the performance is obviously for the benefit of the participants.

For us, in the early sixties, Charlie Dent's morbid, sarcastic cartoons in the *Thresher* were the epitome of Rice students' irreverent, downbeat humor. The best collective example is the Marching Owl Band, affectionately called the "MOB," which came along after my time. In the early sixties the football team was still competitive, and the Rice band was mired in typical paramilitary conformism. But in the seventies the all-volunteer musicians shed their silly uniforms, suppressed their feeble countermarching routines, and transformed themselves into an intentional rather than unintentional parody of a "real" band.

At Rice a sort of self-deprecating humor is literally built in. On several delightfully carved capitals in the cloister of the physics building, completed in 1914, caricatures of actual professors from the earliest years of the Institute peer down at passers-by. On one, William Ward Watkin, the first chairman of the architecture department, sits with his foot on the neck of a groveling student while others bow to him in fear. On another, administrators spin, measure, and cut the thread of knowledge like the Greek fates. A third shows a winged dragon with the face of a professor of chemistry gripping a hapless student in its claws.

I always appreciated these comic architectural touches, which seemed to hint that right at the start, the school and its leading lights were in danger of taking themselves too seriously. At least that's how we saw things when we were students.

The band laced its halftime shows with sarcastic jabs at opposing schools. In the most notorious incident, a MOB routine poking fun at Texas A&M's canine mascot, Reveille, enraged the visiting corps of cadets. At the end of the game angry Aggies surrounded the band in the Rice Stadium fieldhouse. Finally, food delivery trucks were backed up to the fieldhouse doors to extricate the frightened band members—thus saving one MOB from another. The next year, a small East Texas high school returned the application materials Rice had sent, saying that because of the Aggie parody they didn't plan to send any more students to Rice.

—Fryar Calhoun

"Counterball," Baker College Commons

106

Lovett College "Casino Party"

Archi Arts Ball

108

Archi Arts Ball

Archi Arts Ball

On the way to "Night of Decadence"

111

Wiess College "Night of Decadence"

113

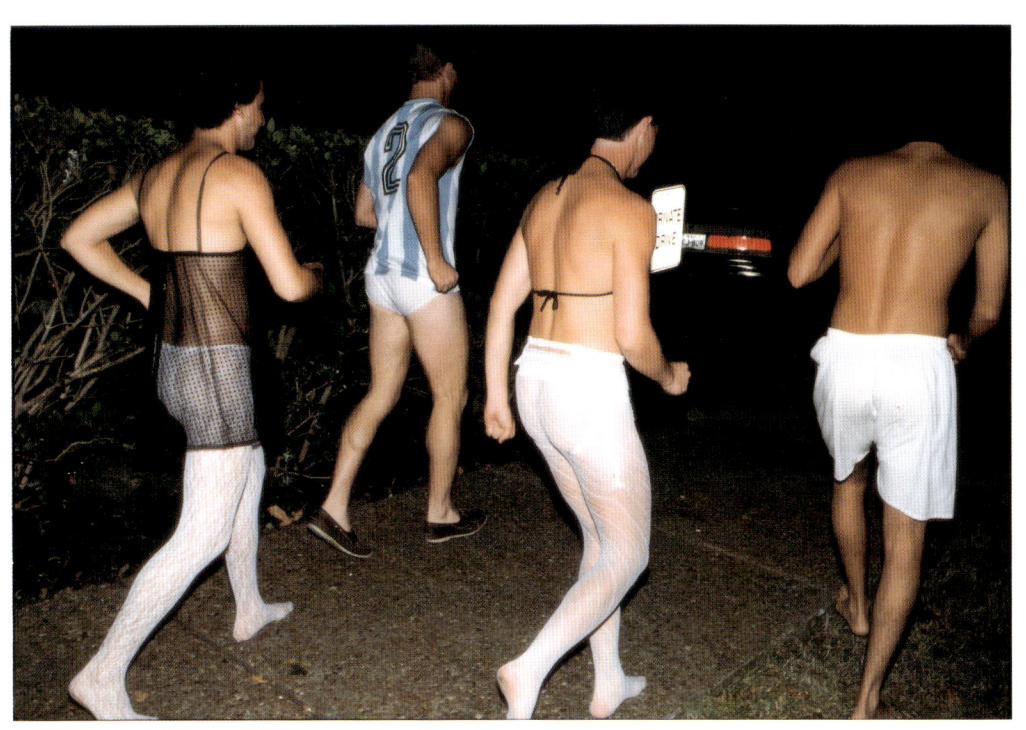

Wiess College "Night of Decadence"

Rice Players' Canterbury Tales

Intramural football

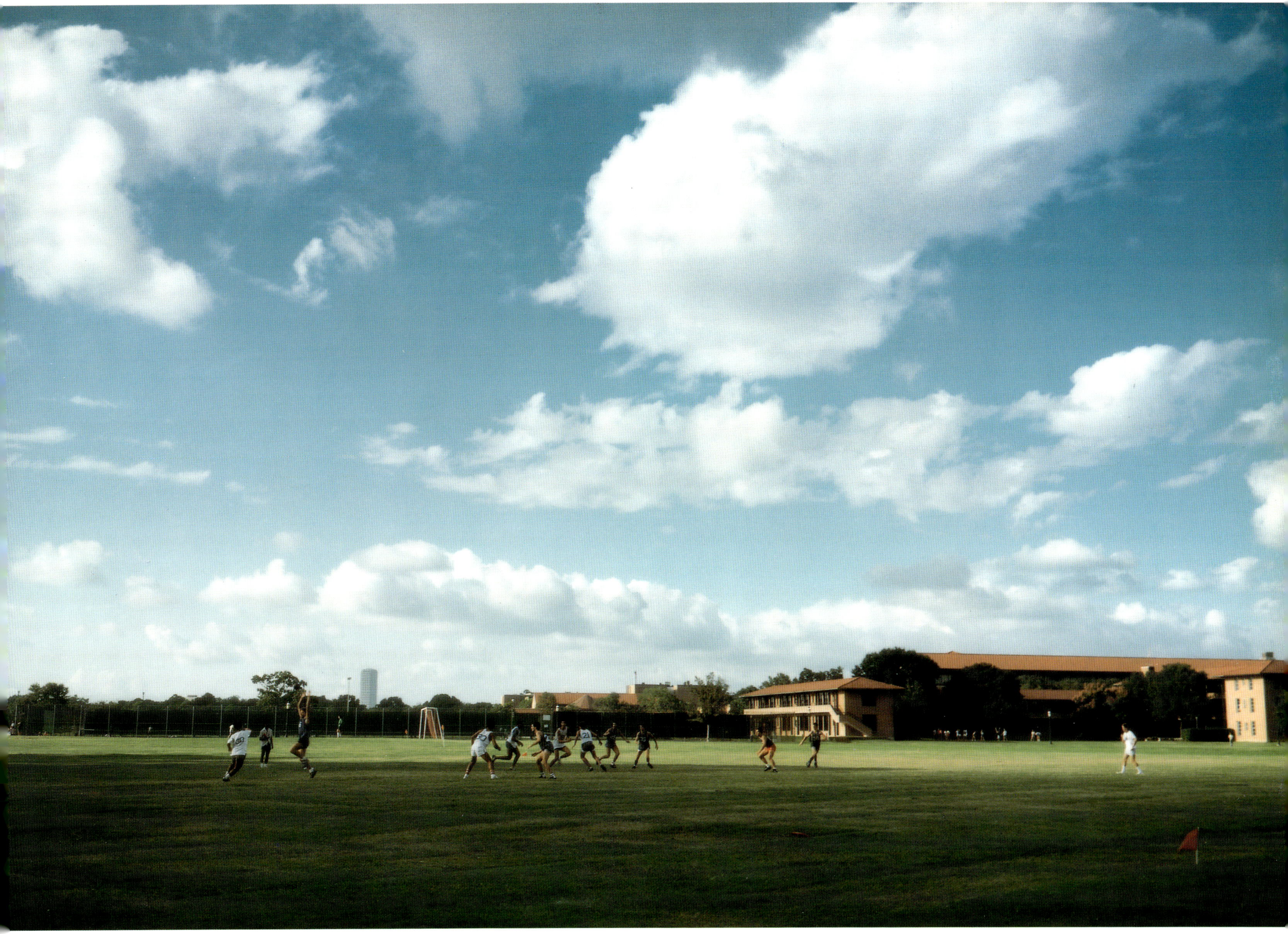

Powder Puff football

Varsity baseball, Cameron Field

Varsity rugby match

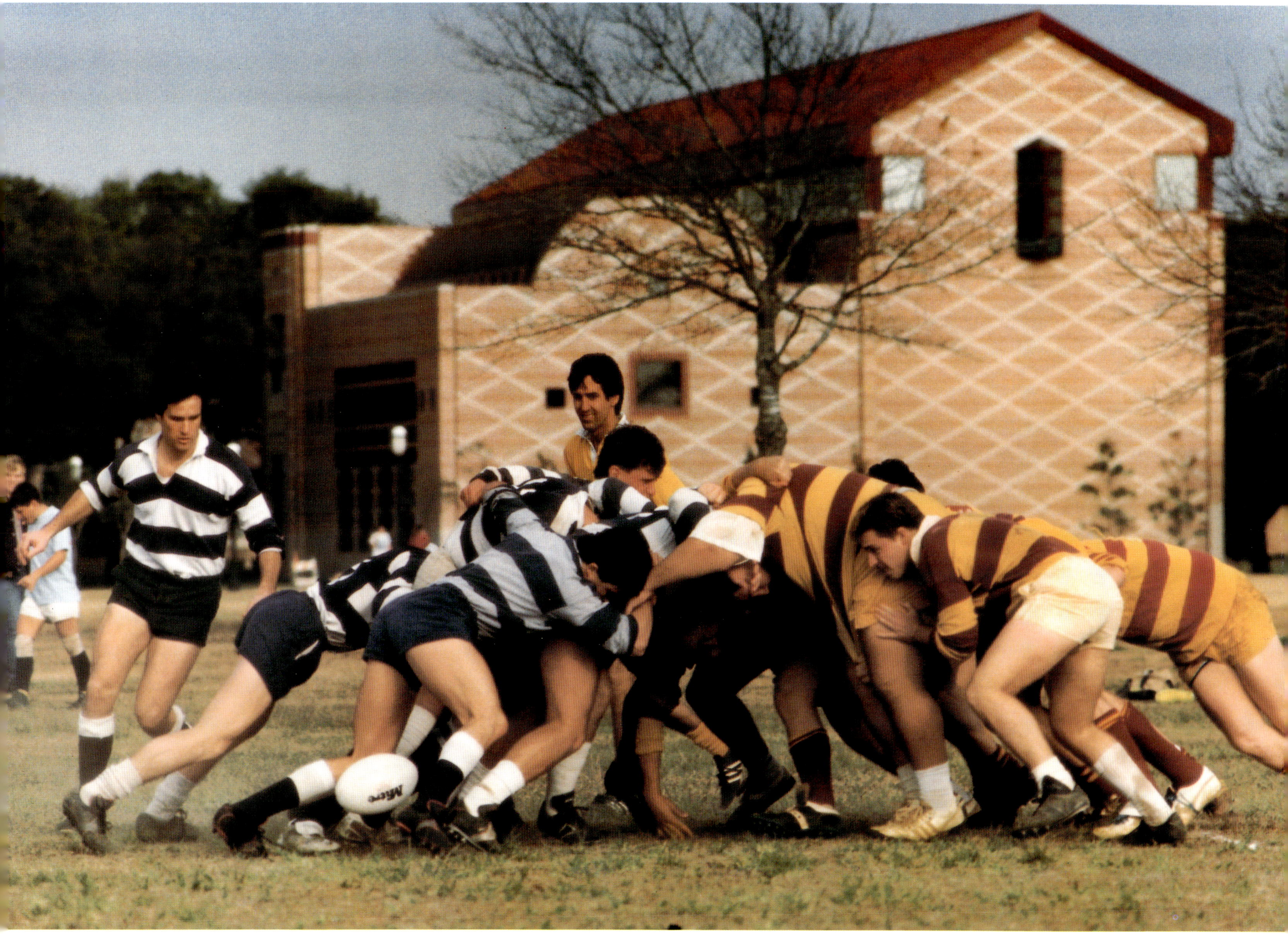

Varsity women's volleyball, Autry Court

Frisbee, academic court

Friday afternoon "TG," Hanszen College quadrangle

Varsity baseball, Cameron Field

Football, Rice Stadium

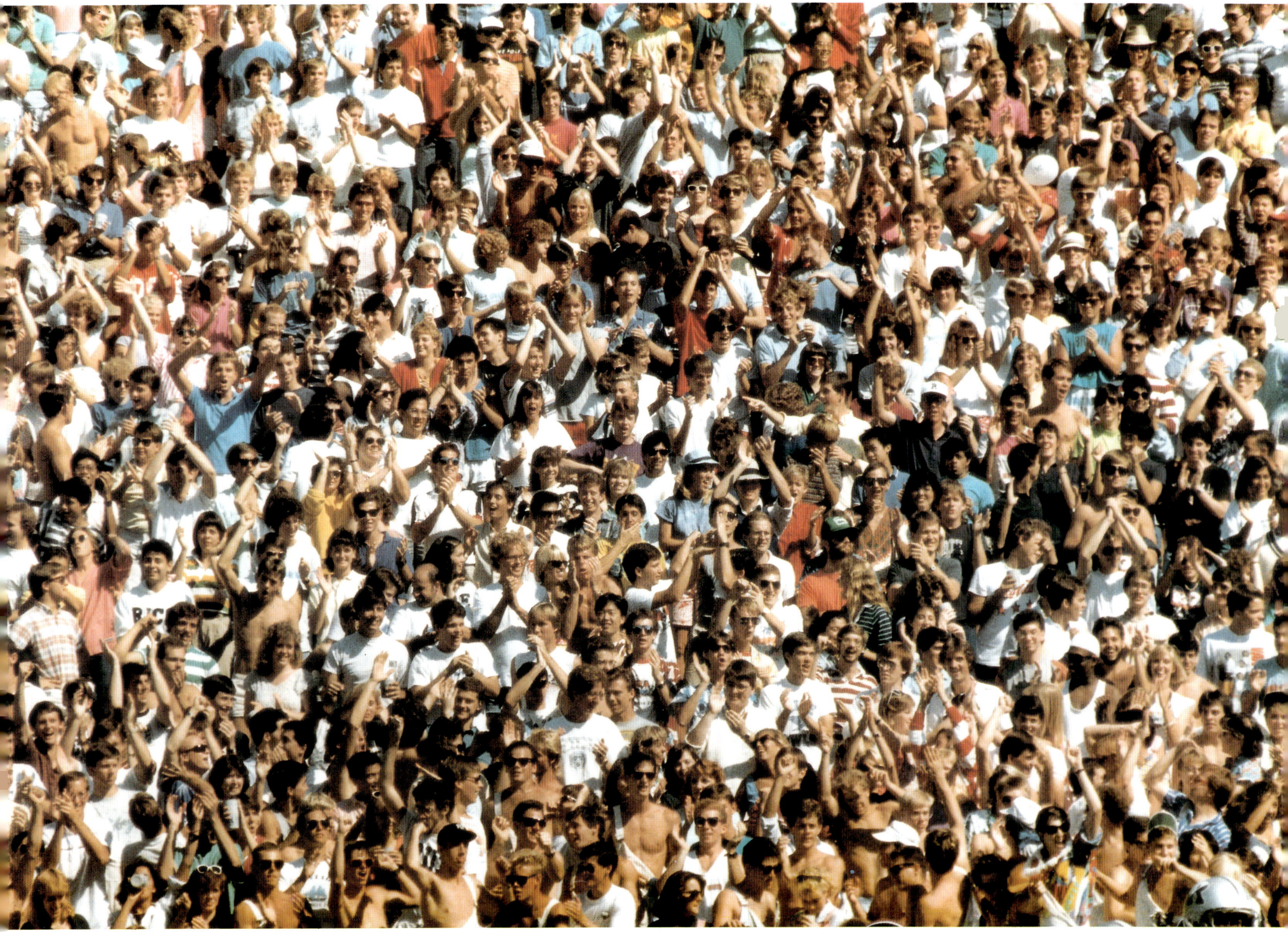

The Marching Owl Band (MOB)

Varsity football, Rice Stadium

Stone carving, Lovett Hall

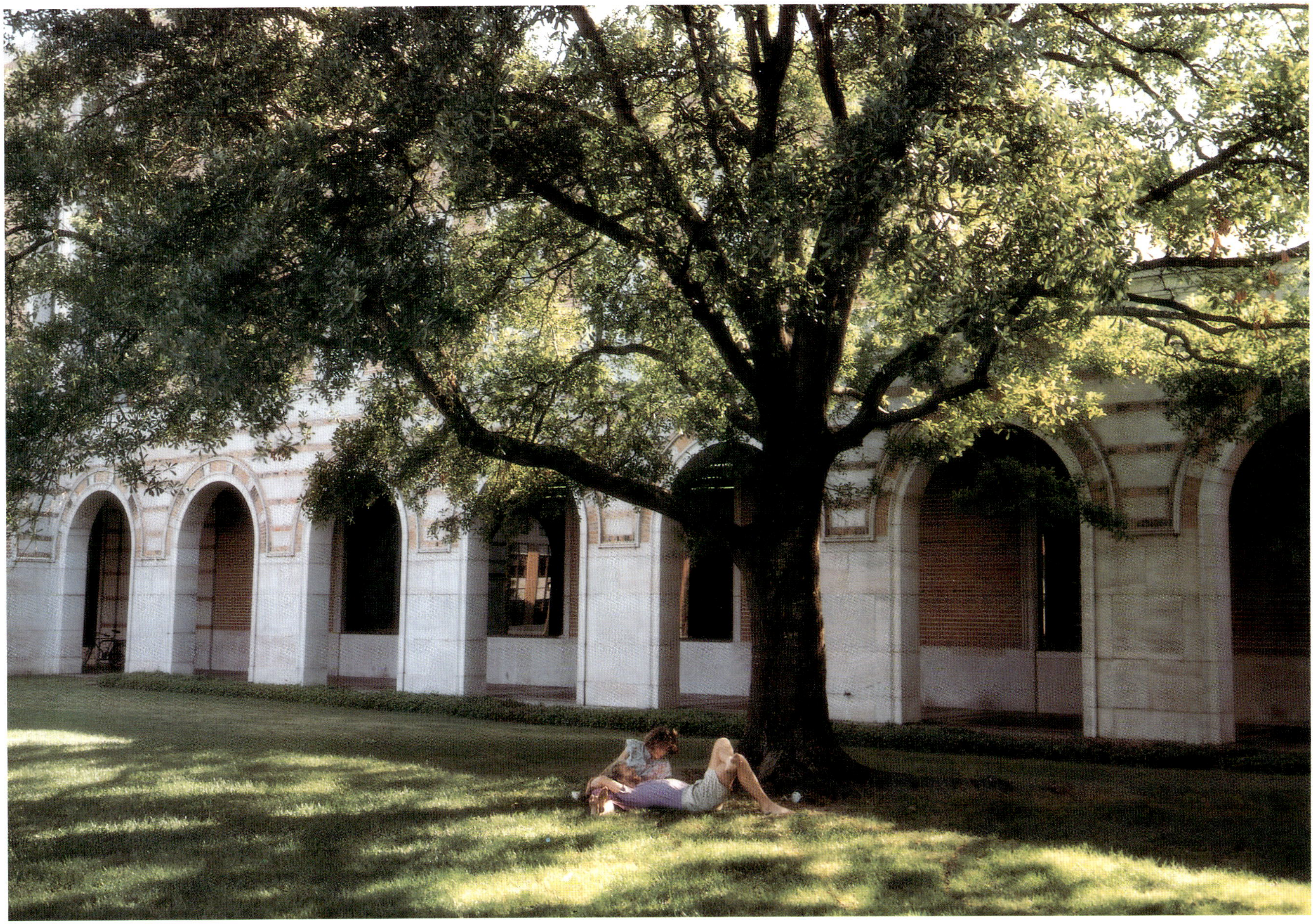

Academic court

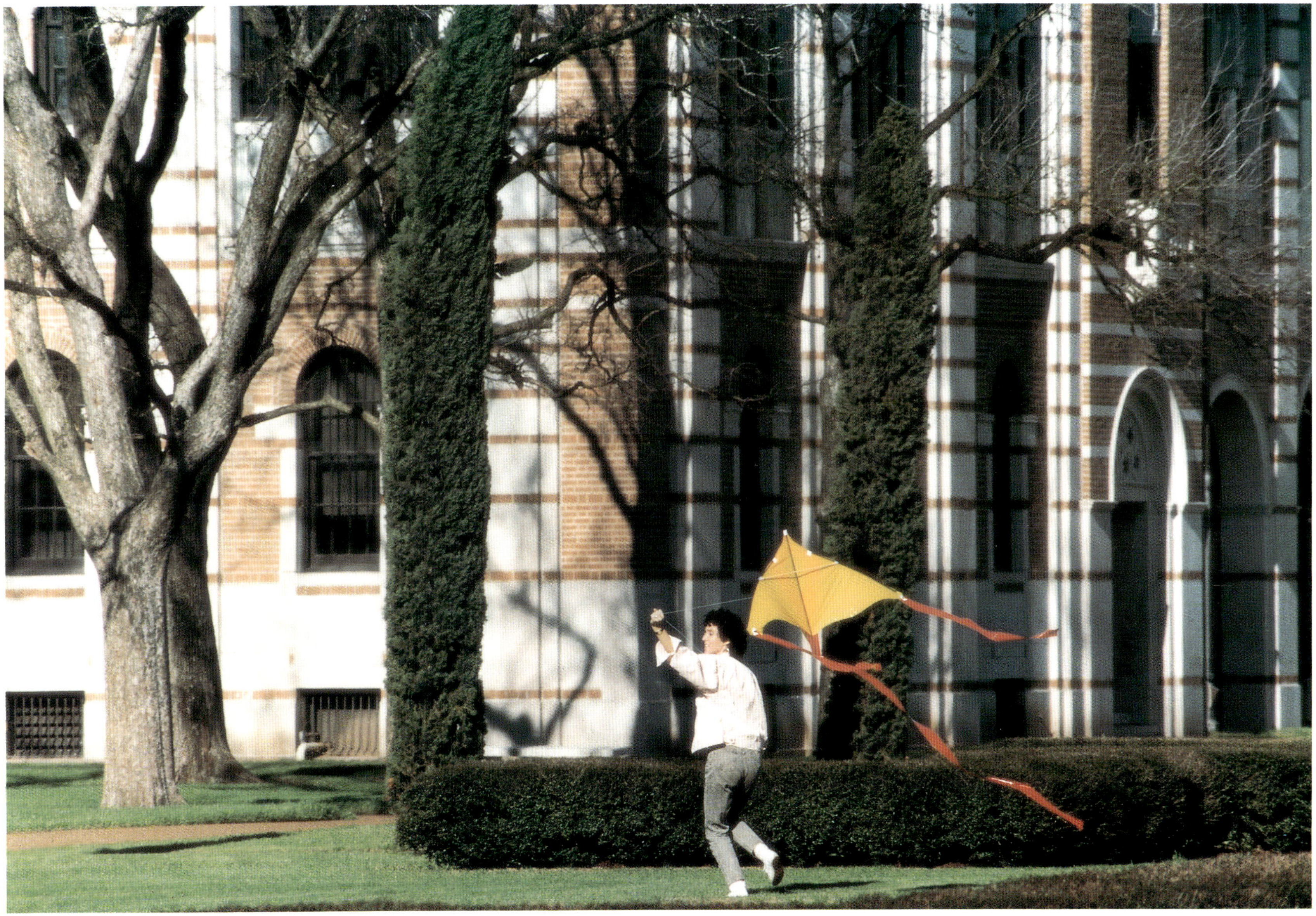

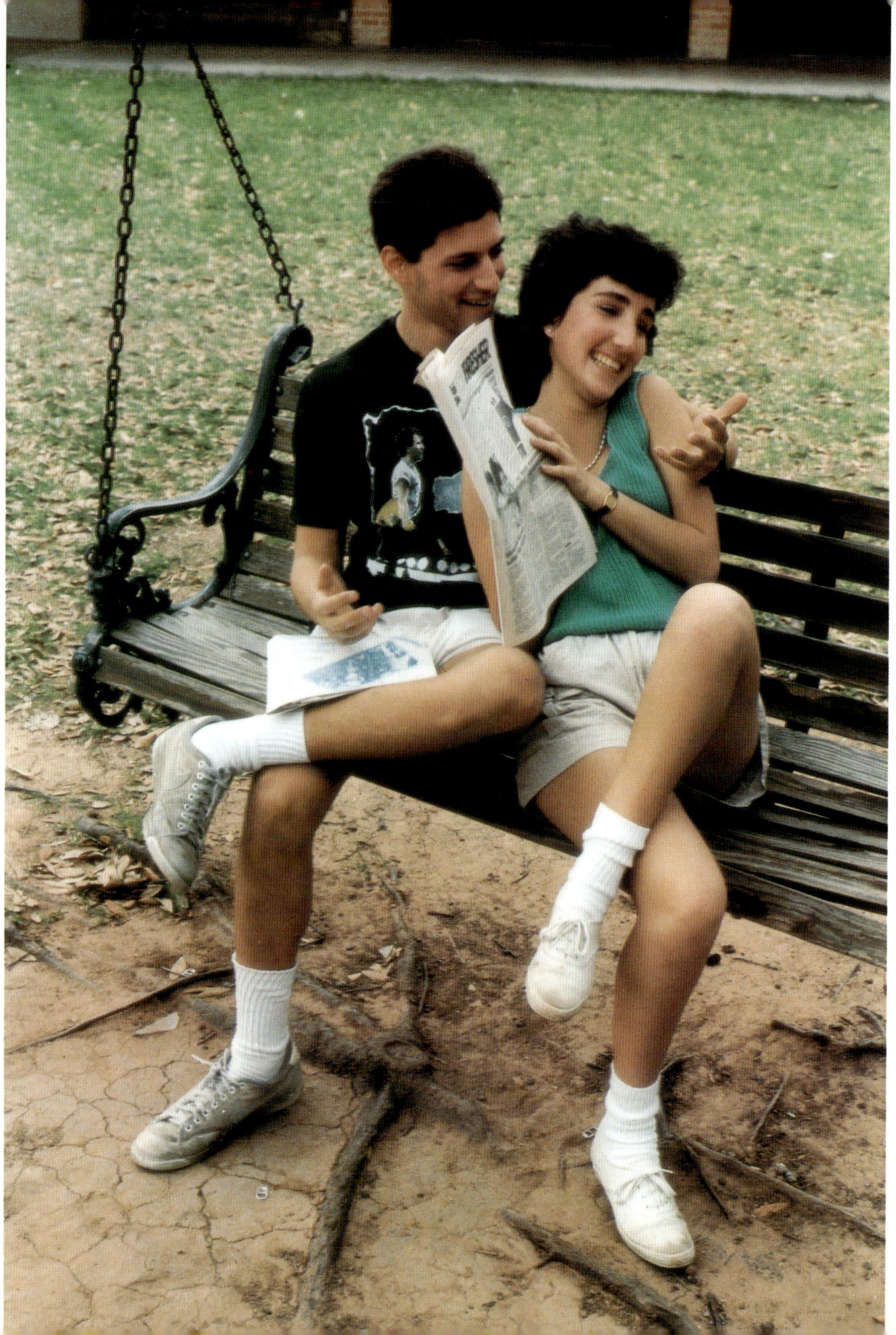

Hanszen College quadrangle

136

King Lear, *Baker College*

Shakespeare Festival, Baker College

Student art exhibition, Sewall Gallery

Shepherd School of Music symphony concert, Jones Hall

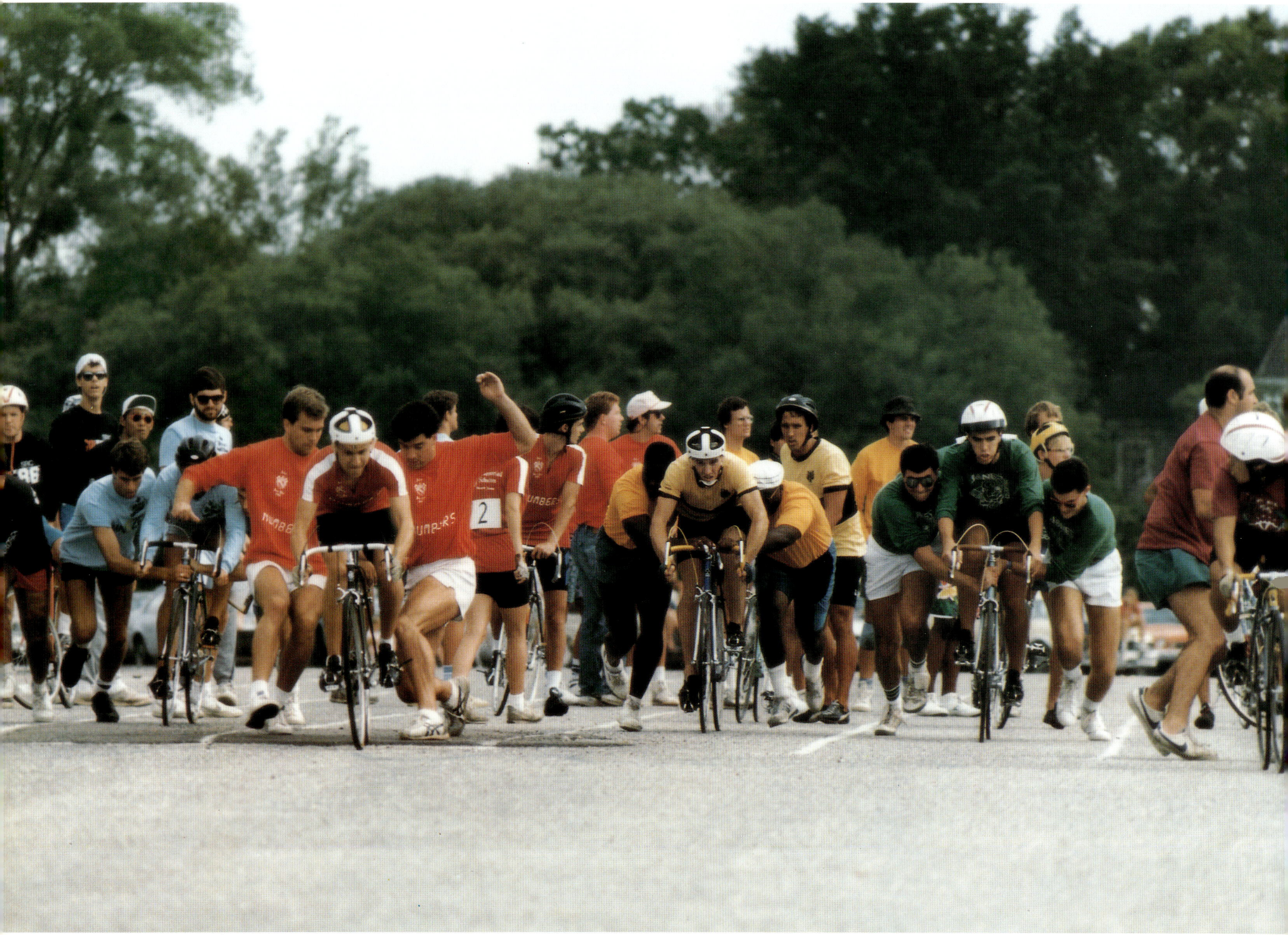
2

Beer-Bike Race

141

Beer-Bike Race

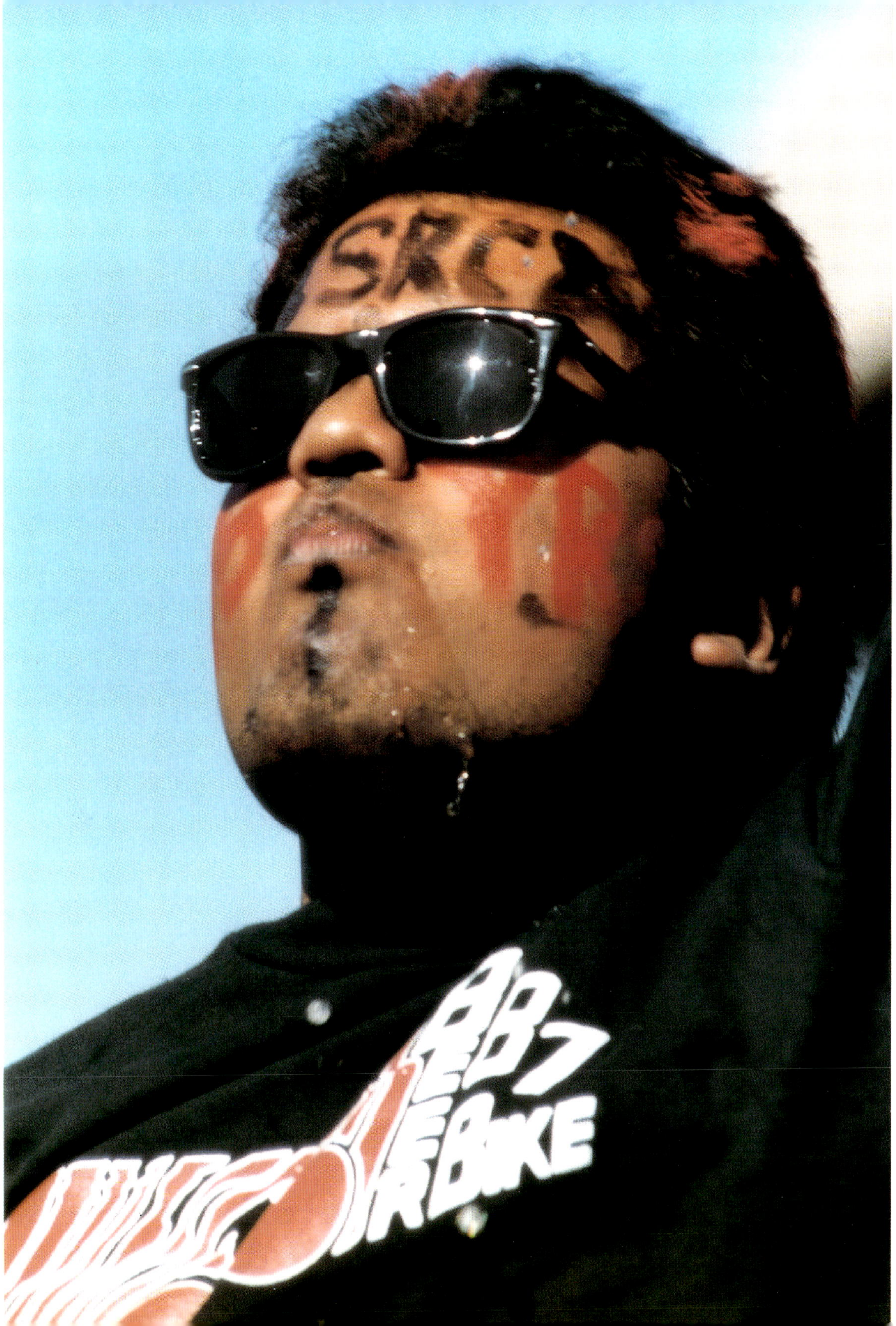

Beer-Bike Race

145

146

A spring day in the academic court

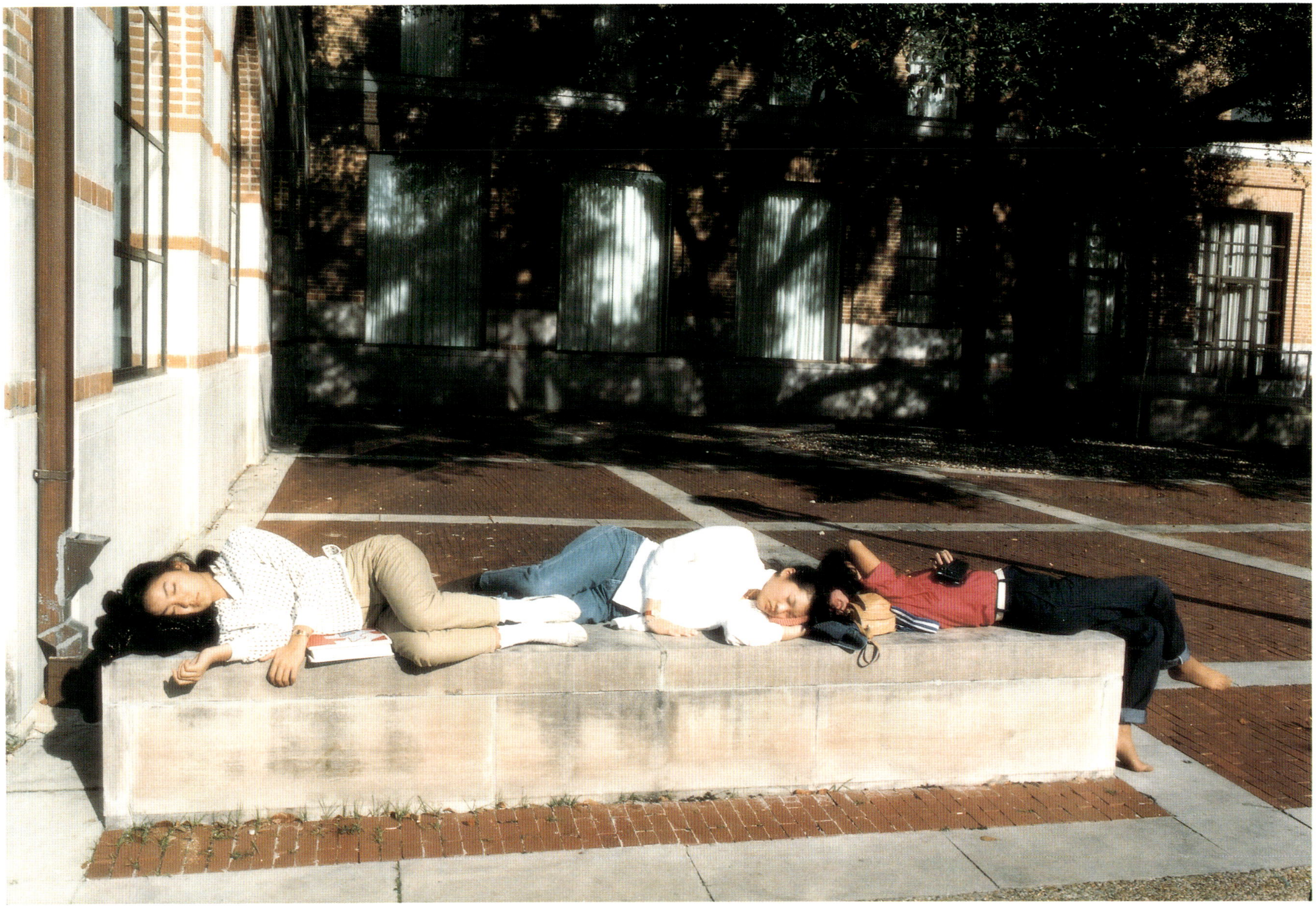

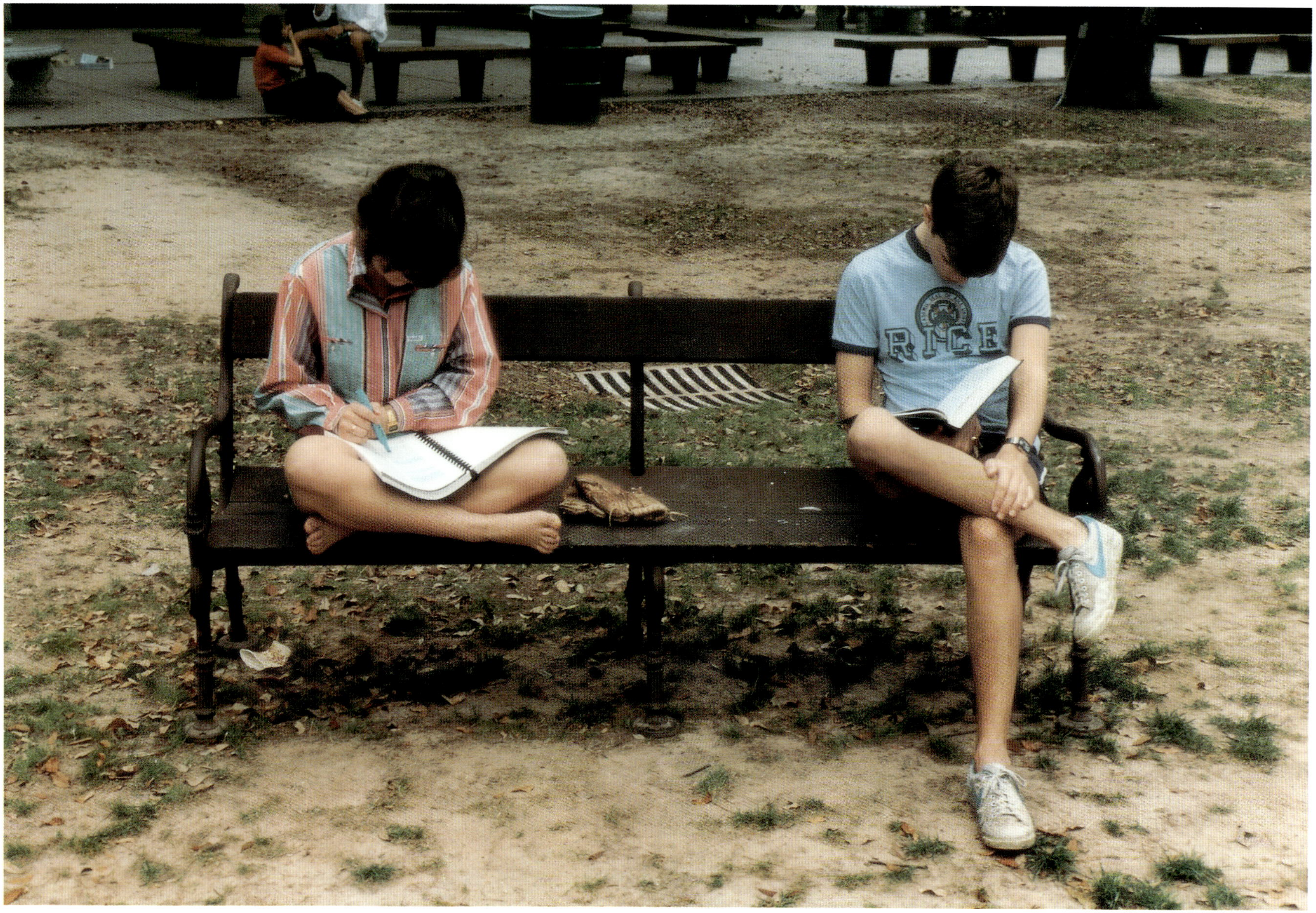
RICE

Hanszen College quadrangle

Under the Sallyport

Heizer sculpture and the Abercrombie Laboratory

Final examinations

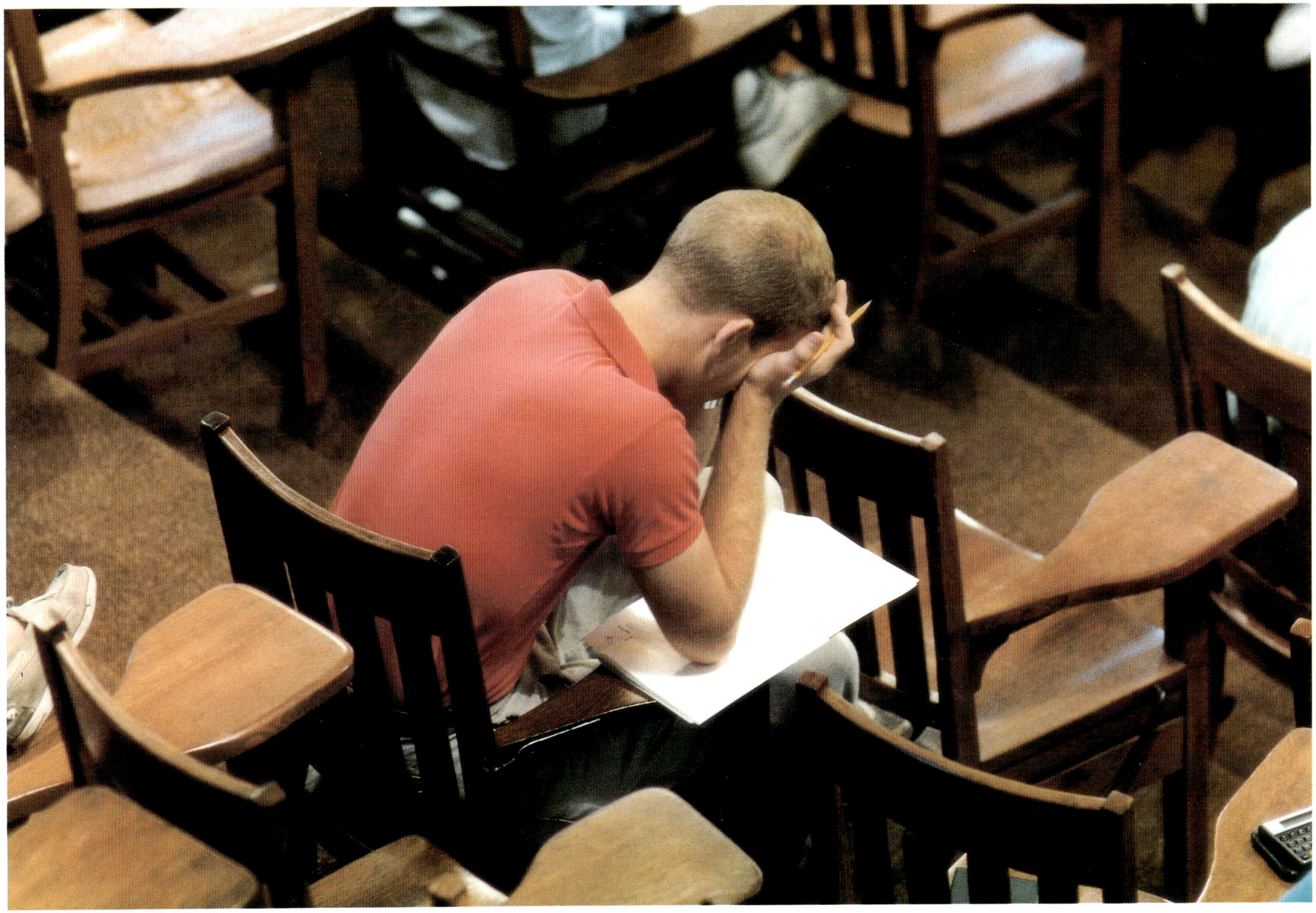

154   *Commencement ceremonies, academic court*

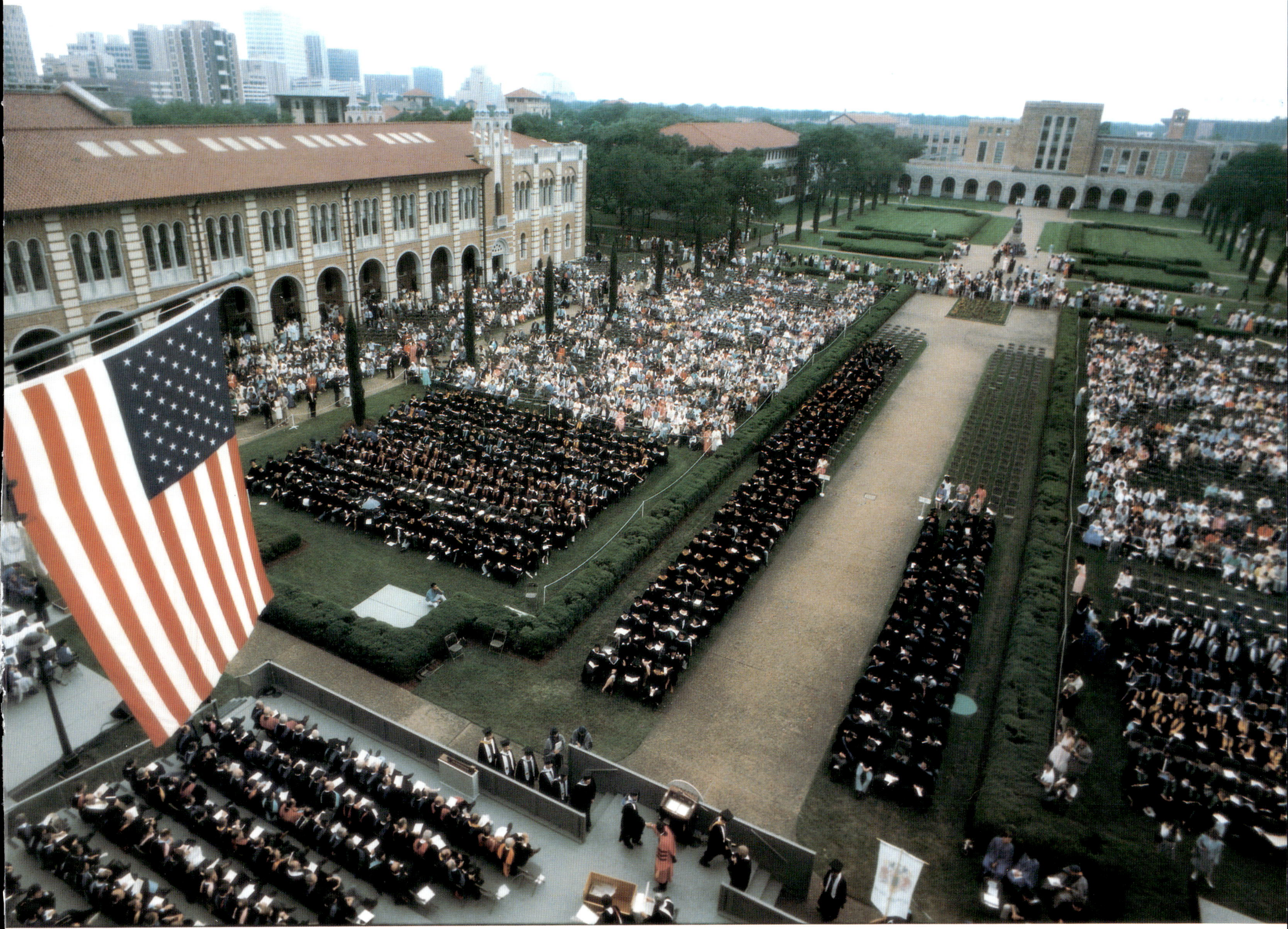

Commencement ceremonies, academic court

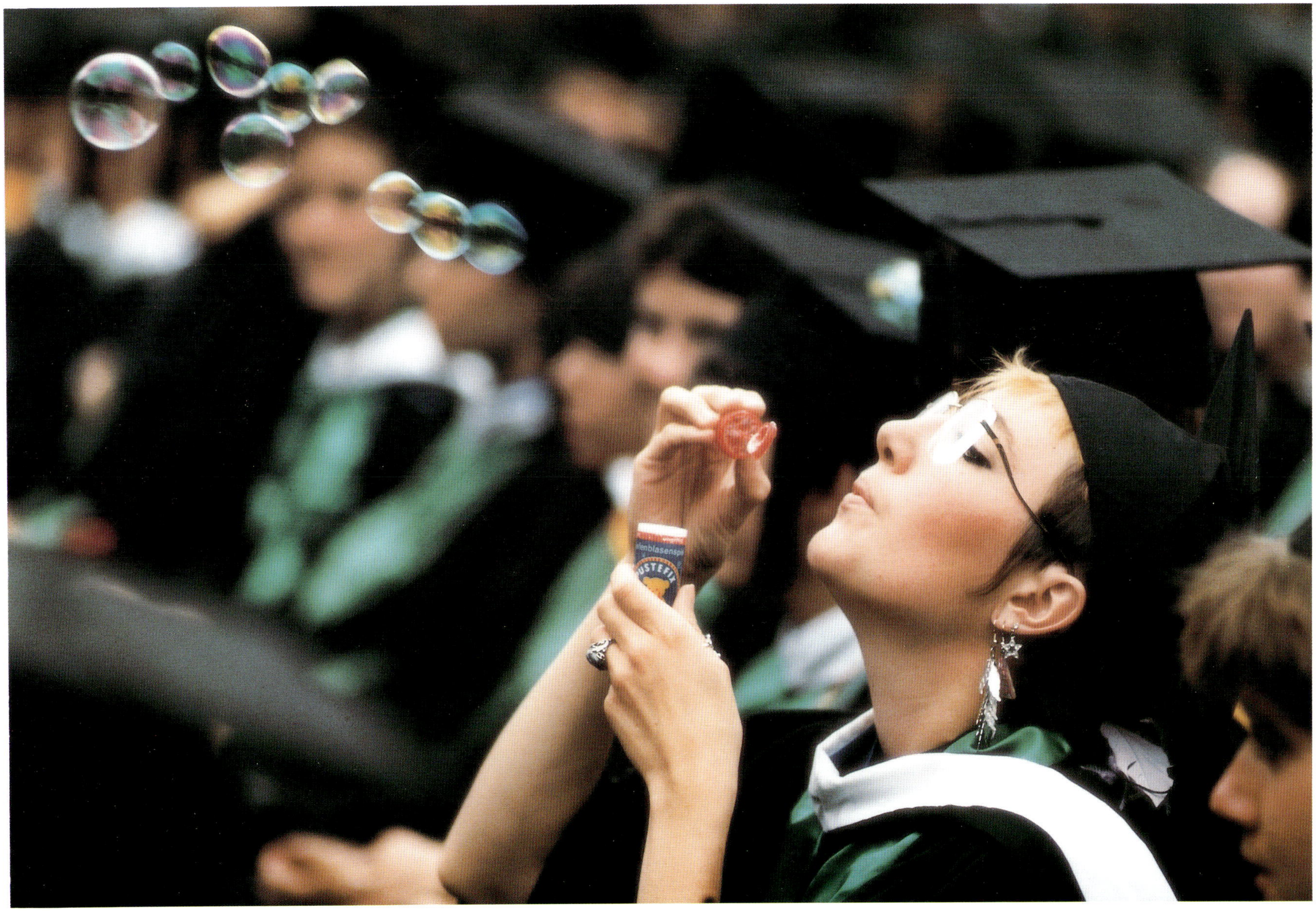

O VISION OF THESE EARLY
DAYS O SPIRIT OF OVR YEARS
OF FAITH O TRVTH & JVST
ICE IN ALLIANCE WITH FREE
DOM SOVL OF ART & SCIENCE
AND BEAVTY TRVTH'S VNDY
ING WRAITH GO WITH OVR
SONS ON ALL THEIR WAYS

Cornerstone, Hanszen College

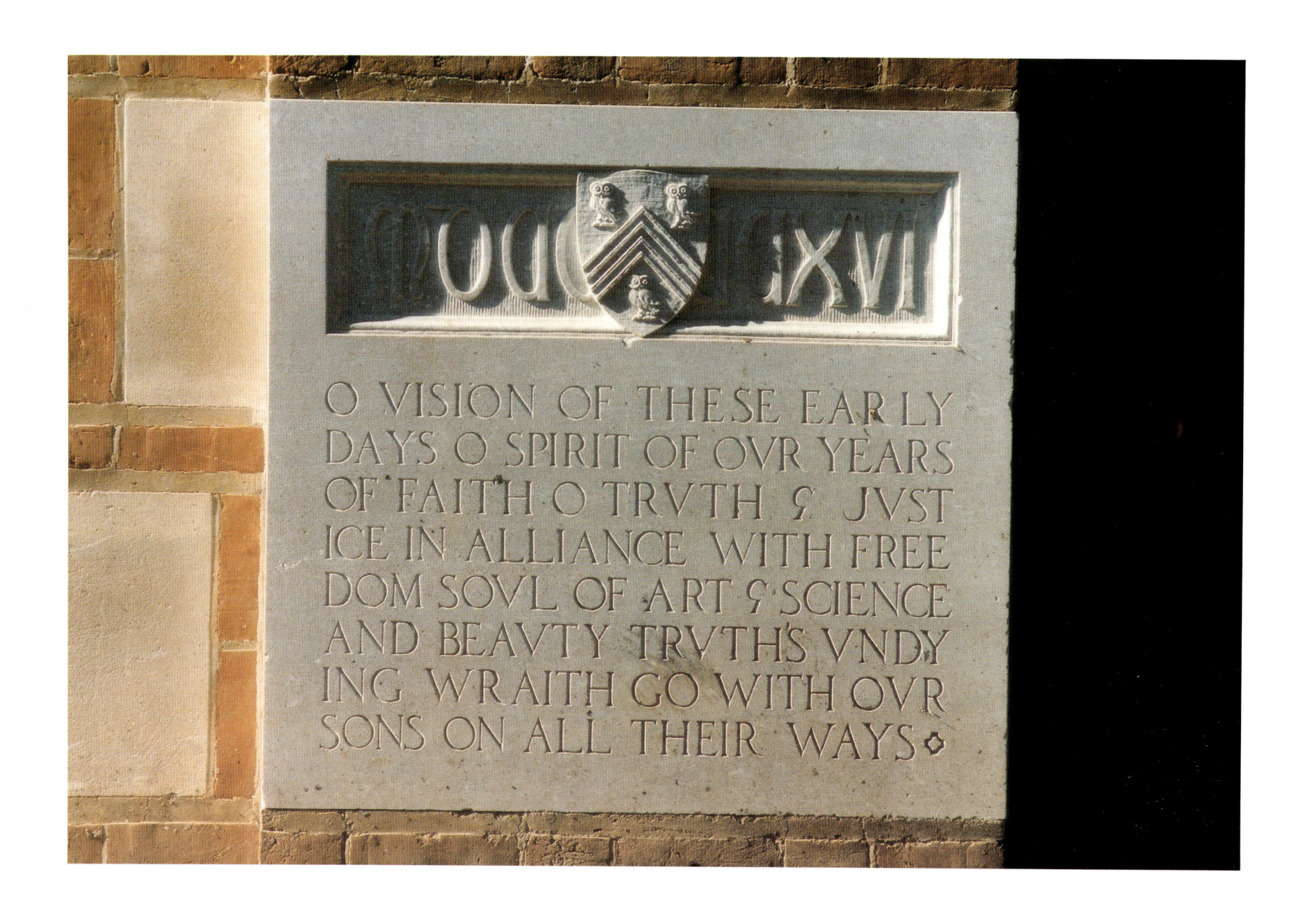

Baker College quadrangle

The photographs of the early construction and opening ceremonies on
pages 5-35 were loaned for reproduction by the Woodson Research Center of
Fondren Library, Rice University. For publication, selenium-toned, silver
prints were made from the original glass plates.

The commentary by Fryar Calhoun appeared in a different form in
Texas Monthly magazine.